FOLLOW
THE FIRE

Steve Gray

Charisma®
HOUSE
Books about Spirit-Led Living

FOLLOW THE FIRE by Steve Gray
Published by Charisma House
A part of Strang Communications Company
600 Rinehart Road
Lake Mary, Florida 32746
www.charismahouse.com

Unless otherwise noted, all Scripture quotations are from the
Holy Bible, New International Version. Copyright © 1973,
1978, 1984, International Bible Society. Used by permission.

Scripture quotations marked KJV are from the King James
Version of the Bible.

Scripture quotations marked NKJV are from the New King
James Version of the Bible. Copyright © 1979, 1980, 1982 by
Thomas Nelson, Inc., publishers. Used by permission.

Cover design by Randall Keeler, Keeler Interactive

Library of Congress Catalog Card Number: 2001092962
International Standard Book Number: 0-88419-785-9

01 02 03 04 05 8 7 6 5 4 3 2 1
Printed in the United States of America

This book is dedicated to:

Eric Nuzum and J. D. King. Like Caleb and Joshua to Moses, both of you have stood with me and encouraged me through the wilderness. May you both help the next generation live out its destiny, as I have had the privilege of leading you in yours.

And to the brave souls who followed the fire from the country to the city, leaving your jobs and property, so that the world could better be served by what God did in our midst.

Acknowledgment:

Appreciation and acknowledgment is given to Joel Kilpatrick, my helper in writing and rewriting so that the world could hear the story.

CONTENTS

CONTENTS

FOREWORD

I have been privileged to watch the Lord shape and mold Steve Gray into a leading voice of revival. When Steve asked for my advice on his plans to move the Smithton Outpouring to Kansas City, Missouri, I could see the Lord positioning the church in a metropolitan area to expand it for world impact.

I had previously visited the Outpouring in Smithton, and now I returned to Kansas City to pray with Steve and his wife, Kathy, on the concrete foundation of their new building. As I stood there, I sensed that the Lord was expanding and intensifying the mandate on Steve's life to bring the message of revival to the world.

What you are about to read is a grand adventure of a

pastor, his wife and family and many other people who left their previous work to follow the fire of revival of God. They left jobs, homes, loved ones and their security to build a revival center in the middle of the country. You will hear their hopes, their dreams and, at times, the despair they faced when the odds seemed stacked against them.

The principles found in this book to maintain and increase the revival have been shared by Steve and Kathy in hundreds of churches and ministries around the world. World Revival Church has become known as a place for burned-out pastors to find their first love and for Christians to be changed by the power of God. From the time you step into the service, you see the hunger the people have for God's glory. The desire and expectation crescendos during worship into the very presence and glory of God filling the room, often bringing people to their knees, weeping. As His glory moves, people are healed, set free and changed.

What distinguishes Steve Gray's ministry? I think it is his strong desire to raise up a people set apart only for God's use. A people who want His presence more than anything else. A people who desire to restore honor to the Lord. Under Steve's leadership, this ministry is being used to raise up a people with the same faith, courage and power that the early church had.

As you read this book, may you be inspired to join Steve Gray and the World Revival Church on your own adventure and follow the fire.

—DR. PAT ROBERTSON
CHAIRMAN AND CEO, THE CHRISTIAN BROADCASTING NETWORK

PART I

ONE

FOLLOWING THE FIRE

I stood on the platform of our church in Kansas City, my eyes filling with tears and my heart with gratitude. Our visiting speaker, John Kilpatrick from Brownsville Assembly of God in Pensacola, Florida, put his arm around me and presented a beautiful wood and brass plaque to my wife, Kathy, and me in celebration of our fifth anniversary of revival. It was inscribed, "From John Kilpatrick and the Brownsville Assembly of God church, to Steve and Kathy Gray, in celebration of five years of revival."

The crowd that night erupted in applause, and for a moment I was at a loss for words. They cheered and whistled, and John led them, smiling broadly at Kathy and me.

Thankfulness surged inside me toward the people and toward the Lord, who seemed to have stopped the constant business of revival long enough for us to appreciate from where we had come.

The crowds had been big that weekend for our annual pastors' conference. People from dozens of states and several dozen churches were among our guests. Hundreds were being blessed and touched by God, and we had planned that evening's program from the order of speakers to the songs the band would play—but this was a moment I had neither planned nor anticipated.

It was a moment that couldn't convey the experience of the trials we had undergone to get to that point. As I looked down at the plaque, the shiny brass surface became something of a window into the recent past, and I began to think of what we had gone through and how far we had come.

When the Smithton Outpouring first began, it brought great liberation to the people in my church and to me. We felt God's love as we hadn't felt it for years. We experienced spontaneity in worship, conviction in the Word, deep repentance and soaring praise. Many times we found ourselves laid out on the floor in awe of God, weeping our guts out or laughing with joy. At other times we danced and jumped so that the floor of our old church began to feel like a trampoline—one that might give way if we pushed it too far.

As a congregation we began to move aside the other things in our schedules—things that used to seem so important and that had commanded our attention for so many years—to make room for the move of God that had entered our church and our lives with billowing clouds of glory.

And yet, in the beginning of revival, we remained a small church in a town of less than six hundred people.

Ours was no urban center, no vacation destination, no city that people might stumble on accidentally. We didn't even show up on most maps. To get to Smithton you had to *want* to get there. There was no traffic light in town, no Coke machine, not even a gas station.

As much as Smithton was a no-name town, I was a no-name pastor. While other people grew megachurches, I had a minichurch. I had no connections to powerful or influential people. No television program . . . no regular traveling ministry . . . no books—nothing. Kathy and I were the only paid staff people at the church, which met in an aging building reminiscent of a Currier and Ives print of a white, clapboard country church.

The people in my church were average, working Americans. We had no superstars, millionaires, converted business leaders, sports figures or city officials in our ranks. We were about as normal as you can possibly get.

Our church and our people had nothing to recommend us to the outside world except what God was doing, which we recognized as being truly remarkable. As His power and presence continued to grow, we realized that He was building something more than a temporary series of meetings. He was building a movement. But none of us knew how far it would go.

The excitement was contagious, and soon people from outside the area started coming, having heard from relatives or friends that "God was in the house." Indeed, God was in the house, and we continued to worship and preach and serve our guests as the number of visitors grew each week. They too experienced the marvelous presence of God. To some it was like cold water in the face—a wake-up call that their life needed to change. To others it was a warm, comforting embrace that restored vibrancy to their souls. To others it was chains rattling loose as addictions were broken. To others it was a healing touch that put their physical bodies right. And to still others it was a call to spiritual battle against darkness.

Each person who walked out after one of our meetings had a different testimony, and those testimonies went forth to all different parts of the country. After a while our visitors were no longer just from Midwestern states, but from further west, further south, further east and even from across the oceans.

Even then we did not know where it would lead. I had no idea that soon I would travel the world and preach in some of the most coveted pulpits in America. Only a couple of years earlier such a thought would have made me laugh. After all, I was an ordinary pastor in an ordinary church preaching to ordinary people.

Back then, the idea that a renowned minister such as John Kilpatrick would speak at *our* church was inconceivable. The revival at Brownsville had changed the spiritual landscape worldwide. Millions were making the pilgrimage to Pensacola, sometimes waiting in line before the sun came up to get into an evening service. I had even been among them.

Now, as I stood on the platform with the plaque in my hands, I was celebrating five years of a revival that not only shook our lives, but has shaken the world, too. It was like a pause in the whirlwind to reflect on from where we had come.

I would never have imagined life could be such an adventure. And I wouldn't have traded a minute of it for the world.

WHOSE FİRE?

The theme of my life and of our revival has become clear to me in recent months. It is the theme of the revival God is giving to the world, a theme that goes back to the very first believers in the Book of Genesis: "Following the Fire."

When you follow the fire you embark on a lifelong adventure unmatched by anything else in the world. It is the only worthwhile adventure—one crafted in heaven just for you.

But it requires much. When you follow the fire, you must:

- Give up your plans to pursue His.

- Change your identity to reflect Christ.

- Build your life around His purpose, not yours.

- Experience times of wandering.

- Leave familiar surroundings behind, not just once but whenever God calls you onward.

- Fix your eyes firmly on the cloud by day and the pillar of fire by night.

- Fight the urge to grumble.

- Deal with opposition and dissension in the ranks.

- Struggle to preserve unity.

- Enjoy the fruit of obedience.

To follow the fire is to accept God's call—specially designed for you and for me. It is a unique adventure, one designed for the people in our generation and to accomplish the specific work God is doing these days. Maybe you are already involved in that work, or maybe you are just being recruited. Before we pass the baton on to the next generation, should the Lord tarry, God wants us to run hard, serve diligently and follow wherever He leads.

No one can begin to imagine where following the fire will lead. But every person alive must decide whose fire he or she will follow. The problem is that many believers, who at one time decided to follow the fire of God whole-heartedly, later decide to trade their remaining embers for a new flame. They have grown bored with God's fire, or it has led them to a difficult place they would rather avoid. For that reason they choose to walk away from it. Others leave to follow strange, ungodly fires.

Others simply refuse to break camp and move on. They are stuck in the desert like nomads, living in constant lack, fighting for whatever sustenance they can find and never feeling a sense of permanence. That happens to people in revival, too. They stop following, perhaps because they have found an oasis they particularly enjoy. Maybe they want to stay with a specific manifestation, feeling or anointing instead of moving on.

The fires of revival can become our own fires if we appropriate them for our own purposes. When we do, we find ourselves confused, left behind the adventure, with only waning coals to warm us.

The question is for you and me: Whose fire will you follow? Whose fire are you following now? Whose desires and purposes light your way? Your own? God's? Your spouse's? Your family's? Your friends'?

Have you chosen to stop following God's fire, or are you still hard on the path?

THE FIRE OF EGYPT

We are not the first generation to follow the fire. The children of Israel were called to follow the fire in the desert—a literal cloud by day and a literal fire by night. Never before had such a thing been seen in the world—a nation led by a column of flame.

It was a sign, a picture of how God would deal with people through the ages. It demonstrated how His presence would lead those who belonged to the family of faith.

Fire is one of the most wonderful images from the Bible, and it is a common image in today's revival, mostly in the context of being baptized with the Holy Spirit and fire. But it is also a symbol of God's leading. The Book of Exodus says:

> And when the cloud was taken up from
> over the tabernacle, the children of Israel went
> onward in all their journeys: But if the cloud were
> not taken up, then they journeyed not till the day
> that it was taken up. For the cloud of the Lord was
> upon the tabernacle by day, and fire was on it by
> night, in the sight of all the house of Israel,
> throughout all their journeys.
> —Exodus 40:36–38, kjv

God's fire was not the only fire they could see. When they began their forty-year journey, the fires of Egypt burned brightly behind them, as if tempting them to return. It would have been easy to stay in the warm comfort of the familiar flames that slavery afforded them. Yes, they had to work hard and endure unfair treatment—but it bought them a place in the most powerful and luxurious society of the day.

Following the fire meant leaving a host of comforts. It meant separating from the protection that came from living under the rule of Egypt. It meant leaving an abundant source of food. It meant leaving permanent homes and shelters. It meant losing access to the markets and trade of Egypt. It even meant losing easy access to water.

For all that they did wrong, the children of Israel made it over one of the biggest hurdles: leaving the fire of the world and taking the first step toward the fire of God.

WE WALK BY FAITH

Like many believers, Kathy and I had been following the fire of God as best we knew how for years before revival came. We had come to the Lord right after college, been baptized in the Holy Spirit and eventually began traveling and ministering with a music group. Our evangelistic ministry was growing, and we were becoming successful by all outward appearances. But it got to the point where I knew something was missing. The fires we were following had left me cold—I had a strange chill in my spirit.

I first noticed it in 1981 when we were traveling and ministering. One night, after a particularly good service, I felt hollow when I should have felt warm and full of satisfaction. That night many were saved and filled with God's Spirit—a "successful" night of ministry by anybody's standards. But I felt empty on the inside. It would have been easy to attribute my feelings to the devil or to weariness, but the feelings persisted and began to grow stronger. Deep in my heart was a longing for a true revival that would change the face of Christianity.

I felt the same as I imagine some Hebrews felt when word got out that they would be leaving Egypt. There was a stirring inside of me that spoke of new adventures, but also new dangers. I was giddy, but also uncertain. The ministry we had built was good, but I knew the fire of God was moving, and I desperately wanted to follow it. If we continued camping out where we were, we would be surrendering our future and settling for our own fires, which, though they comforted us, lacked power.

Driving down secluded highways in our Greyhound bus late at night, I would grapple with my feelings. There was a gnawing in my stomach for something more that I could not fully explain. Like most traveling ministers, I had grown tired of preaching to pews filled with people who had only a limited interest in the things of God. I had grown weary of pastors who had to offer gimmicks and giveaways to get their own congregations to attend church. What had happened to many churches? Why had luke-warmness become the order of the day? Why did people care about politics, stocks, sports, school, television, movies, computers, business, vacations and food more than the things of God? Who redefined what church should be? And where were the firebrands for God? Where were the people whose one desire was to stand in the presence of the Lord? It was so rare to see someone truly committed to Christ. If you saw them one time, it was likely that the next time you ran into them they would have the glazed-eye look that many Christians had, indicating that they had given in, lost the fire of their early passion and become a card-carrying member of the "Part-time Christianity" club.

I didn't want to hear any more excuses for why someone couldn't be in church. I didn't want to hear the pastor apologize for low attendance on Sunday nights. I wanted to live as the men and women had lived in the historic revivals of Wales, Cane Ridge and Azusa Street. I wanted to see the Book of Acts in action, not just on paper. Reading about past revivals sent thrills down my spine, and I began to believe that God was going to do it again.

The fire is returning, I thought. *Let it come.*

THE ROAD TO SMİTHTON

Revival was almost a foreign concept back in the early eighties, the days of church growth. Megachurches were springing up all over the country, and not many saw the need for a revival of radical, New Testament-type proportions. After all, the Christian community was gaining power and prestige in political circles, starting radio and television stations, building a bustling Christian music scene. The number of evangelicals in America was said to be growing, and by all accounts the church appeared to be on the march toward victory. Weren't we in revival already?

Churches may have been experiencing success of some kind, but it was not the visitation from God that was burning in my heart. I felt estranged from the successes of those days. I felt as if my season had not come, and at times I feared it never would. The Charismatic movement was booming, as evidenced by the magazines, music and massive conventions people were attending across America. But what I saw with my natural eyes did not exactly match what I saw with my spiritual eyes. I wanted to see a brush-fire revival that would visit, not convention halls and coliseums, but local congregations, local altars, where the servant-leaders of revival would be normal pastors and normal Christians with the touch of the Holy Spirit on them to do great works.

I talked about it so much that one night Kathy sheepishly suggested that we stop traveling and that I become a pastor. "Oh no, not that," I said. "I don't want to go through what I see hundreds of pastors going through—dying in the trenches, getting beaten up by their own congregations, slowly wilting without ever making a mark on their communities. As traveling ministers we have the advantage of leaving town after a few days, and that keeps us from getting hurt."

But Kathy's words stuck with me. The more I thought about her suggestion, the more I warmed to the idea. I desperately did not want to miss a move of God, so I began looking for opportunities to become part of a local congregation. Eventually she convinced me. If I wanted to really see God in action, I would have to yield to the idea. I schemed that perhaps a pastor somewhere would resign right after I arrived in town, and I would be the logical choice to succeed him.

Finally, partly out of fear that I would miss the revival,

I made a drastic decision to go home and wait on God for an answer. We canceled our schedule—a bold move for a young couple who had just begun to make it. We had a full schedule of churches booked in advance for the entire year. The number of people receiving salvation was at an all-time high, and so were the offerings.

But we left it to follow the fire.

THE NEW PEOPLE OF GOD

Following the fire causes people to do things that appear illogical to unbelievers or to believers who have lost their fire. But sometimes that is what it takes to be obedient. I'm sure that when the children of Israel packed up camp to follow the cloud by day, it didn't always make sense to their heads. But their journey was of the Spirit—not the flesh, and so it is with us today.

This is one of those precious times in history when the kingdom of God breaks in with dramatic power to transform the religious system of the day. Maybe you have experienced that power, or maybe you have only heard about it from someone else. Maybe your church is part of the revival, and maybe it is resisting it.

Whether we like it or not, this is a day of choosing. The kingdom is near—what will we do with it?

Jesus began His ministry by announcing the nearness of the kingdom. It was the responsibility of the hearer to respond, often with radical change. The fault line in the Gospels runs between those who heeded the call to righteousness and those who didn't.

Think of Zacchaeus scurrying down the tree to take Jesus to dinner at his home. All of a sudden it didn't matter how many people he had cheated, stolen from or lied to. The past became irrelevant the moment Jesus called his name, and Zacchaeus found himself among those who responded correctly to the kingdom.

Think of the disciples who left their nets, their plans and their tax booths. Mary left a life of prostitution; the Samaritan woman left a life of sin. These people whom society would have called average, boring or ungifted have become examples of making the right choice.

When the kingdom comes near, God chooses unlikely people—the unnoticed and the outcast—to fulfill His will. I was one of them. Are you? Do you fit in that crowd of followers who had nothing to recommend them, but who made the most important choice of their life to follow the Savior as He walked the earth?

In our day we are experiencing a fresh fire of the Spirit. It is burning up many of our old religious blueprints. When Jesus went to Jerusalem He found corruption and greed at the temple and in the hearts of God's people, especially the leaders. What does He find today? Whose blueprints are we following—blueprints that do not match the King's? What are we trying to build outside the scope of His plan?

To follow the fire is to lay down our plans, no matter how precious they have become to us. God is demanding people who do not try to mix old and new plans, who aren't tacking God's ideas onto their lives like an extra room in the house. They are willing to see every other thing they have built razed to the ground so that His kingdom can be built in their midst.

HEARING THE CALL

Our response will decide whether we succeed or fail in His plans. In the blaze of today's fire of the Lord, ordinary pew-warmers are being transformed into firebrands for the Lord. They are adjusting everything in their lives to accommodate the King. People who had nothing going for them other than a good job and a nice family are suddenly being catapulted into positions of leadership. They have gone from a regular seat on the third pew to the front lines of battle.

But others have not responded at all, or they responded for a little while and then gave up. They went from being on fire to lukewarm to cold. They went from the third pew to the back door.

The present-day visitation of God is forcing us out of our nonresponsiveness. I don't see much middle ground; to follow the fire of God we must follow—get up, move, step forward, get in the flow!

Jesus' story of the rich man and Lazarus from Luke gives us a clue as to how we should respond. It is a well-known parable:

There was a rich man who was dressed in purple and fine linen and lived in luxury every day. At his gate was laid a beggar named Lazarus, covered with sores and longing to eat what fell from the rich man's table. Even the dogs came and licked his sores.

The time came when the beggar died and the angels carried him to Abraham's side. The rich man also died and was buried. In hell, where he was in torment, he looked up and saw Abraham far away, with Lazarus by his side. So he called to him, "Father Abraham, have pity on me and send Lazarus to dip the tip of his finger in water and cool my tongue, because I am in agony in this fire."

But Abraham replied, "Son, remember that in your lifetime you received your good things, while Lazarus received bad things, but now he is

*comforted here and you are in agony. And besides
all this, between us and you a great chasm has
been fixed, so that those who want to go
from here to you cannot, nor can anyone
cross over from there to us."*

*He answered, "Then I beg you, father,
send Lazarus to my father's house, for I have five
brothers. Let him warn them, so that they will not
also come to this place of torment."*

*Abraham replied, "They have Moses and
the Prophets; let them listen to them."*

*"No, father Abraham," he said, "but if someone
from the dead goes to them, they will repent."*

*He said to him, "If they do not listen to Moses
and the Prophets, they will not be convinced even
if someone rises from the dead."*
—LUKE 16:19–31

As with many of Jesus' parables, the end of the story
presented a complete reversal of prevailing Jewish opinion.
The religious leaders would have thought that since the
rich man was blessed by God on earth, certainly he would
be blessed in eternity. And certainly the poor beggar, they
would have thought, must have brought his plight on himself by sinning, so surely he would go to hell. But Jesus'
story surprised them—it ended the other way around.

This parable is one of many that Jesus told to empha-
size His main ministry theme: The kingdom of God is
near. Some people who seem to have it all together will
miss the kingdom, and some who seem to have nothing
going for them will find it. Christians should really be

much more sobered than they are by these stories. Many times we automatically assume that God would treat us just like the poor man—but who's to say He would not consider us to be like the rich man?

Preachers have a tendency to cut many of Jesus' parables short so the ending fits the theme of their sermons, but like many of His stories, this one had a disquieting conclusion. It didn't end with the two men realizing they were separated by a chasm—it ended with a plea from the rich man to warn his brothers. Suddenly it was no longer just about two dead men, but about five living men. The rich man, realizing his fate was sealed, interceded for his brothers so they wouldn't have to go to hell. But Abraham would not grant the rich man's request. He said that all the brothers had to do was listen to Moses and the prophets, and they would go to heaven.

The rich man represented Israel in Jesus' day. The people of Israel had Moses and the prophets, but they were no longer listening to God, no longer following the fire. Abraham even told the rich man that if someone came back from the dead to tell his brothers about their end, the brothers would not listen.

How this message cuts into the very heart of churches today! Not long after He told this parable, Jesus Himself was killed and laid in the grave. Three days later He came back from the dead. We now have the witness of a man raised from the dead—more than the rich man's brothers had—and so many still do not believe.

Even worse, Christians hear the call to live for God alone, and they hesitate, having lost their ability to respond. What sermon is left to hear? What plea from heaven have they not understood? Even a miracle resurrection will not convince some believers. The kingdom has come near, but they have no ability left to respond to the call.

The words of Stephen as he spoke to the stony hearts of

the religious leaders just before they stoned him still ring true today: "You are just like your fathers. You always resist the Holy Spirit!" (Acts 7:51). Just like those who prayed to heaven in Jesus' day, many of us know how to appear spiritual and yet resist the blaze of revival at the same time. We know how to kneel at an altar time after time, often in tears, yet never change the direction or focus of our lives. We have learned how to sing each line of the songs of revival and never let the words penetrate our stony hearts.

We have Moses and the prophets—and the Son of God who was raised from the dead—and still many are not convinced that total commitment is the way to go. It is the sin of neglect that condemns. While Jesus stands with both arms stretched toward us, we neglect to grab hold with all of our might.

HIS FIRE

Whose fire are you following? What does it take for your heart to be pierced? Do you live in confusion, always questioning your purpose, restlessly changing jobs, hobbies, homes or cities? What fire illuminates your way? Is it the dark, dreary fire of personal ambition and self-serving? Or is it the bright, clear fire of God?

In the coming chapters I will lay out a plan to help you start following the fire of God more fully. It will not be easy. It will challenge you to the core of your beliefs. That's the point. The fire of God is sent to uproot you from where you are, to show you how to lead a life worthy of the One who has called you.

That's where the adventure begins. It starts when we start—by leaving behind our personal Egypts and following the fire wherever it leads.

EXCHANGING OUR IDENTITY FOR HIS

If someone had to stick a big label on you describing who you are, what would the label say? That you go to church a lot? That you are faithful to your job? Your husband? Your children? That you have terrific grandchildren and a well-kept yard?

What if you could scratch away the layers of your identity one layer at a time? On the top would be surface habits—you like chocolate or pizza or quiet evenings at home. You like nice cars and reading about military history. You like needlepoint and taking walks in the evening with your neighbors.

Keep scratching, and you find opinions and beliefs—you think the country would be better if a certain political party were in office. You are concerned that children don't have respect for their parents any longer. You wish there were more wholesome programs on television.

Scratch even deeper, and you find the core identity of a person—the hardwood under the layers of varnish and paint. Few people see you at this level, perhaps only your spouse and a few close friends.

This is the level that may reveal you are fundamentally a compassionate person—but it also reveals deep insecurities and a desire to be loved at any cost.

It reveals fears that have been bred into us, and joys that are so fulfilling we have difficulty describing them.

Each of us has that level of hardwood, those traits and beliefs that stay with us through life. Each of us could point our finger at certain traits we appreciate and other traits we would rather get rid of. Some are part of our genetic package, and some come from experience. Now and again each of us wonders: *Who has defined me? Who shaped my beliefs? What is my identity?*

The good news for all of us is that God offers a trade-in program—our identity for His. The Bible says:

> *I have been crucified with Christ and I no longer live, but Christ lives in me. The life I live in the body, I live by faith in the Son of God, who loved me and gave himself for me.*
> —GALATIANS 2:20

This does not mean that just one day you gave your life to Christ and were "crucified" on that day. No, Paul said:

> *I die every day—I mean that, brothers—just as surely as I glory over you in Christ Jesus our Lord.*
> —1 CORINTHIANS 15:31

He further clarified our daily crucifixion by saying:

*We always carry around in our body the
death of Jesus, so that the life of Jesus may also
be revealed in our body.*
—2 Corinthians 4:10

Trading our identity for Christ's identity is a daily thing. And it goes beyond what most Christians think.

I like to say that the hope of the ages is for some unknown, forgotten or despised man or woman with nothing left to lose who surrenders everything he or she has to God and follows the fire. These people take a wholehearted plunge into a new identity.

History books reserve space for people who are so lost in a cause that it becomes their identity—and their lives light the way for millions of others.

Martin Luther was that way.

So was the apostle Paul.

Martin Luther King . . .

Mother Theresa . . .

Francis of Assisi . . .

Billy Graham . . .

How many men and women can you think of who have shaped the world in which we live today? You don't even have to be a Christian to make an impact on the world. Just believe something and follow it single-mindedly as Gandhi did, and future generations will honor you.

But any cause except that of Christ and His kingdom is mere foolishness. It is nothing. It is less than nothing. Yet a majority of Christians muddle through life without ever experiencing the adventure of following the eternal flame.

One reason is because many are so busy wearing multiple identities. They never come close to the realm of greatness because they want to be too many people. Open their spiritual wallets, and you find multiple pieces of identification, each giving a different description.

Yes, we like to go to church, but we are not willing to make following the fire of God our first priority. Yes, we are moved by Christ's sacrifice, but we wouldn't consider sacrificing everything we have for Him.

The problem is this: Following the fire requires a singleness of identity. The kingdom of God thrives on integrity and a focused, sincere effort. It withers in the presence of multiple agendas. Such a person is "a double-minded man, unstable in all he does" (James 1:8).

Double-mindedness—having dual identities—is one of the primary plagues of the church today.

CHANGING "NORMAL"

I'm convinced that a lot of whom you become as a Christian is the result of whom you hung around in the first year after you were saved. The vast majority of us hung around at least some people who were part of the church for reasons other than the fact that they loved Jesus. Maybe they were looking for a spouse. Maybe they were locked in a religious tradition in which rules were most important. Those traits have been reproduced in countless lives today.

Contrast these Christians with people who are saved during moves of God. At our church we have observed that "revival converts" have a totally different definition of "normal." They do not become accustomed to attending church just once or twice a week because we go four and five times a week. They never get used to a one-hour service because revival services last about three hours. If you wrap the service up in an hour, the people feel cheated! On Friday and Saturday nights, revival converts show up for revival services because that's the only kind of church they know.

But it is much more difficult for someone who has

grown up with all the "normal" church habits to change when God demands more. There may not have been anything wrong with the church they were in or with the people who shaped their characters, but now God is trying to do something new and fresh in the land, and they're locked up in the old definition of normal. Some people can't even enjoy new music because their mind tells them that God only moves during songs they sang as a child.

To move ahead in revival you need to let God change you, or you will fall behind.

GAİNİNG HİS İDENTİTY

We cannot gain the privileges of the kingdom without exchanging our identities for the identity of Christ. Kingdom privileges are reserved for kingdom people—and kingdom people carry the identity of the King, Christ Jesus. Only those who go through with the identity change can claim kingdom privileges.

Before my wife, Kathy, and I were married, she had her own name, her own life and her own identity. Even though we were dating and spent a lot of time together, our identities had not changed. I was still Steve, the single guy, and she was my girlfriend.

As we grew to love each other, I would have gladly shared with her anything and everything I owned. But that sincere love and close relationship did not enable Kathy to go into my bank and withdraw money from my account. She might have stood at the teller window explaining how close our relationship was, how we just went out for ice cream the night before and how she believed that one day we would get married, but it would not have made a difference. Her name carried no authority when it came to my bank account. Likewise, I couldn't walk into her bank and withdraw funds from her account, no matter how much I tried to charm the tellers.

Then Kathy and I were engaged. Still, we had no legal right to make claims to anything the other person owned. That only happened on the day we got married. The day she gave up her name and took on my name, the day I became her legal husband, Kathy could take as much money out of my bank account as she wanted, and I from her account.

It was not enough to just say my name; she had to *change her identity* to obtain the rights and privileges my name carries.

This is a picture of how the gospel works. We are supposed to trade in our old selves and be made new in Christ. We receive sonship and take on His name.

But Christians today do not understand the identity change. They think it only takes a whispered prayer and a secret commitment, perhaps made at the altar of a summer youth camp, to bring kingdom power into our lives. Some people go back to a certain moment—one single moment in all of their lives—when they said the sinner's prayer. That, they think, makes them a permanent member of God's family, even if the life that follows looks nothing like Christ.

Real believers have undergone an identity change. They have sacrificed who they were and can say as Paul did, "I no longer live, but Christ lives in me" (Gal. 2:20). That's when we begin to feel the life and power of Christ surging through us, and His Spirit becomes our motivating force. When you submit to the identity change, you feel alive like never before.

İSRAEL'S İDENTİTY CHANGE

God has always been in the business of changing people's identities. Abram became Abraham. Sarai became Sarah. Jacob became Israel after a pivotal visit from God. Saul of Tarsus became Paul the Apostle.

Even the nation of Israel underwent a major identity

change when the children of Israel began following the fire. To help them make the identity change, God gave them new rules. Imagine waking up one day to the news that God was going to give you a new set of rules, rules that would govern every aspect of your life from how you prepared food to how you settled matters of justice and how you worshiped. That is what happened when God gave the Law through Moses.

Everything changed for the Israelites when the Law was given. The Israelites had already left life as they knew it in Egypt, and they were living in the open desert at the time. Now God was telling them to abandon nearly every cultural or societal habit to which they had grown accustomed over the past several hundred years. It was one of the most profound identity changes in history.

In the ensuing centuries, after they finally made it to the Promised Land, the children of Israel often slid back into their old identities, shrugging off the commands of God and identifying themselves with the world around them. They worshiped idols and abandoned God's rules for living. The entire Bible, in fact, is about a people struggling to hold on to its new identity in Christ.

Do you struggle to hold your identity in Christ? Do you find yourself slipping back into the old ways? Maybe you think it's not worth it—but I'm here to tell you that it is! It's worth everything you can give—and more.

"IN JESUS' NAME"?

Most people don't understand the identity change that believing in Christ requires. Many try to appropriate the promises of God without following through on their pledge to give their lives to Him. Many churches allow people to live by their own ideas and opinions, yet teach them to end prayers with "in Jesus' name," as if that brands them as His followers. But that tag is mere words.

It gives a feeling of security, of rightness, of having the proper identity. But that tag is not worth anything if our lives don't reflect His identity.

The seven sons of Sceva tried the "in Jesus' name" trick and got into hot water with a demonized man. (See Acts 19:13–16.) They tried to cast out demons by invoking the name of Jesus. The demons said, "Jesus I know, and I know about Paul, but who are you?", and left the men naked and bleeding (vv. 15–16). The sons of Sceva had called on the name of Jesus without identifying with Him, and the results were disastrous.

The disciples, by contrast, had sufficiently lost their own identities to call upon the name of the Lord and perform many miracles. They didn't just appropriate the tag—they appropriated the identity.

When David fought Goliath, he said, "I don't come against you in my name. I don't come against you with a sword or a spear," meaning he wasn't coming in Saul's name either, but rather, "I come against you in the name of the LORD Almighty" (1 Sam. 17:45). God honored the fact that David was willing to lose himself in God, and He gave David victory over the giant.

Jesus also said, "Where two or three are gathered in My name, I am there in the midst of them" (Matt. 18:20, NKJV). Gathering in Jesus' name means more than throwing two or three people together and praying in Jesus' name. It takes more than that to open the windows of heaven. It doesn't work that way. You can have two or three, or two or three million, people gathered. You could fill every stadium in America with people, but you haven't gathered in *His* name until you have lost *your* name. God wants those two or three—or two or three million—to have the same identity.

If you and two or three other people will humbly join together with a fervent desire to lose your own identities and take on His name, He will certainly be there—you can count on it! The fires of revival will burn brightly, and the world around you will begin to change.

A NEW CONNECTION

Having a new identity means leaving our old identity behind and forging a new connection with God. In Genesis 12:1, God told Abraham:

Leave your country, your people and your father's household and go to the land I will show you.

The faith of Abraham began with a willingness to disconnect from his former life. He was willing to deny himself long before Jesus spoke those very words to His disciples.

It is so important that as Christians we understand the concept of denying ourselves. Some of us think it means cutting back on television or not eating chocolate. But denying ourselves doesn't mean becoming less worldly—it means *disconnecting from who we once were.*

The call of Abraham and the call of Christ were very much the same, and the same call goes out to every person of faith: We are to leave what we know to follow God's plan. Through faith we disconnect from our former lives, ambitions, plans and habits, denying them a place of power or influence over who we are now. We go forth connected to Christ.

The Bible calls this *adoption,* which is leaving your old identity and connecting with a new one. As believers, we receive the spirit of sonship, or the spirit of adoption, and we cry, "Abba, Father" (Rom. 8:15). A person who has been adopted may know about his former life, but he has no connection to it. If God has adopted you, you are His dependent, and you inherit the power and authority of His house.

Many sincere Christians are living in frustration because they are trying to find themselves rather than lose themselves. Jesus taught us that the man or woman who loses his life will find it, and the one who finds it will lose it (Matt. 10:39). Many people spend their lives trying to find themselves. Every day on television or in magazines you can hear people say, "I have to go away to find myself." That is the opposite of what the Bible says to do.

Of course, the goal is not to live lost but to be found in Him. But we cannot *reconnect* with Christ until we *disconnect* from what came before. We cannot arrive somewhere new if we never leave where we began.

The calling of Elisha is a good illustration. (See 1 Kings 19:19–21.) Elijah threw his cloak around young Elisha, who then slaughtered his oxen, burned the plow and set out to follow Elijah. He left nothing to go back to. He did not take a few oxen with him "just in case."

There are some people today who would consider Elisha's act foolish, just as they would consider Peter foolish for dropping his net and Matthew foolish for leaving his tax collection booth. But taking on the identity of Christ means disconnecting from our old identity, our old ways, and leaving no avenue open for return.

THE İDENTİTY SHİFT

When you connect to Christ and identify with Him, you become an enemy of the world. But you may be surprised to learn that identifying with Christ also makes you an enemy of many people *inside the church*. Why? Because some who are posing under Christ's identity have not really lost their own identities. I find this sad fact to be all too true.

Before I became a believer, one church in my hometown often asked me to sing a special song in their Sunday morning service. I would say yes, even though I spent the Saturday evening before playing music in a bar. I went to church on Sunday to sing a special song with my head hurting, my eyes red from lack of sleep and my breath smelling like breath mints because I was trying to cover up the stench of what I had drunk the night before. Yet the people loved me. They didn't care about my lifestyle. They just cared that I could sing. As long as I agreed to sing on Sunday morning, they let me keep my Saturday night routine.

Then I got saved and filled with the Holy Spirit, and I began to believe in the power of God. That same church needed somebody to help them out, and they hired me as an assistant to the pastor because I was on fire for God. But as time passed they didn't like me as much. Now, instead of being spaced out on worldly things I was following hard after God. My mind was clear, my heart pure. I felt cleansed and light on the inside. I was taking on the identity of Christ.

But apparently that wasn't what they wanted. I was a safe, known commodity when I came in with hangovers and sang "The Jericho Road." But now that I was living on the Jericho road, people thought I was too radical.

Eventually they told me, "We think it would be in the best interests of your career if you would leave." That was probably the best advice I have ever received—prophetic, even.

The identity changes that happen to us as we take on the identity of Christ can be confrontational and condemning to another believer who is not willing to make the radical identity change that God requires. As revival hit Smithton Community Church and many of our members began a transformation into the identity of Christ, others in the church grew resentful and left the church. The identity change that God was bringing to some was upsetting to others. As we followed hard after God, becoming more like Him as much as we could, the change didn't sit well with certain people. That's when we learned that true friends are those who support what God does in your life. Your enemies are the ones who pressure you to maintain an old identity.

The same will be true of you. Some people will like you better when you were less radical, less committed, less on fire. They will want the "old you" back.

I think of the time when Jesus healed the demoniac who lived among the graves and cut himself with stones. (See Mark 5:1–17.) The people of his town witnessed his transformation from a naked, raving lunatic to a clothed, sane man—and their response was to ask Jesus to leave! Apparently they were more comfortable with the man's former identity than with his new, God-honoring identity.

A LIFE ON LOAN

Our culture tells us that our identity is determined by what we own, which products we use and how much money we make. We equate identity with ownership. We are the sum of our assets, our stock value, our savings, our IRAs and our treasury bonds. The ultimate life would be one in which you no longer have to work to make a living.

Jesus talked about such a man in Luke 12:13. As Jesus was walking along, someone in the crowd said to Him, "Teacher, tell my brother to divide the inheritance with me." We can assume that if a man in the crowd was asking for arbitration of a family dispute, he was too poor to have any other resources. Rich people don't yell at passing teachers to settle their problems.

Interestingly, Jesus responded with a story not about poor people, but about a rich person:

> Then he said to them, "Watch out!
> Be on your guard against all kinds of greed; a
> man's life does not consist in the abundance of his
> possessions." And he told them this parable:

"The ground of a certain rich man produced a good crop. He thought to himself, 'What shall I do? I have no place to store my crops.'

"Then he said, 'This is what I'll do. I will tear down my barns and build bigger ones, and there I will store all my grain and my goods. And I'll say to myself, "You have plenty of good things laid up for many years. Take life easy; eat, drink and be merry."'

"But God said to him, 'You fool! This very night your life will be demanded from you. Then who will get what you have prepared for yourself?'

"This is how it will be with anyone who stores up things for himself but is not rich toward God."
—Luke 12:15–21

The man in the crowd wanted Jesus to settle a dispute over an inheritance, but Jesus went after the root problem: greed. He told a story about a rich man to the poor man as a warning that greed can reside in any heart, rich or poor. He was rebutting the prevailing attitude that wealth solves problems.

He painted a picture of a man whose identity was wrapped up in his possessions. One year this man had a bumper crop—the equivalent of winning the lottery, for it allowed him to not work for many years if he so wished. But God demanded his life that very night.

What was the man's mistake? Was it not working hard and growing a crop? Not storing it away in barns? No, his mistake was in his attitude—*he thought he owned his life.*

Like most of us, he was busy fitting all the pieces together, making his plans, when suddenly reality broke through. His life was over. It had been recalled, effective immediately. Everything he thought he possessed—including his next heartbeat—was gone.

One of life's great illusions is that we have ownership. We think we own our lives, our houses, our cars, our things. We think we own the property on which we live, even though twenty, fifty or one hundred years ago it belonged to someone else. Whatever you say is yours will belong to somebody else someday—your house, your possessions, your jewelry. It's an illusion that you can grab anything and call it your own.

Indeed, Jesus' parable is not about a wicked man. It's about a typical man who was thinking as most people think. Everything we have, including life, is on temporary loan, and when the loan is called back, we will have to give an account, an inventory, an explanation for everything. The point of the parable is this: Start living your life as if it is on loan to you. You don't own it—God does. He has loaned it to you for a season and a reason.

When that truth becomes part of your identity, you will live more carefully, with forethought and wisdom. You will build character before bank accounts. You will invest in God's plans rather than your own.

You will start to follow *His* fire.

Jesus ends the parable by saying that we need to be rich toward God. I can tell when people are rich toward God because they are generous to everyone. People who are always grabbing for things are poor. They feel they need every ounce and more of what they earn. They are always scrambling for more. They may be rich in possessions, but they're poor because they can't bless anybody else.

People who are rich in God can afford to serve the

Lord. They aren't bound by what they think they need. People who are poor in God always need something to fill their sense of emptiness. They can't afford to be in church because they need to go to the mall or to the movies or to spend time at home. When you are rich in God, you can afford to be in church as much as you want.

God looks at the bare wood underneath our varnish of Christianity. That is where our identity is revealed. Not in our many words. Not in a commitment made long ago.

Does heaven look at your life and identify you with His plans, His life, His victories and His persecutions? Are you clothed with Christ? Crucified with Him? You cannot have a double identity and please God. Revival will only work for you if your identity is fully in Christ. Then the storehouses of heaven will open when you pray. You will have the right to do business transactions in the kingdom of God because you wear His identity, not your own. All the promises of the Bible will come true for you, and the rumored glory will manifest in your life.

Why do we exchange our identity for His? Because His is so much better!

THREE

THE REDEFINED PEOPLE OF GOD

▼

I can still picture the inside of that classroom in my hometown in Missouri. Silence ruled as thirty or so students put pencils to paper and tried to answer the test questions correctly. There I sat, pencil poised above the paper, sweat beginning to pop out all over my forehead, my mind trying to summon the answers I had crammed into it during the class period before.

Invariably, on test day, the same thought would float through my brain: *I hope she grades this one on the curve!*

The curve was a life-saving measure that some brilliant teacher had devised to rescue people like me from certain failure. Instead of grading my score against a fixed number, the teacher added the highest and lowest scores and divided it by the number of people who took the test.

Average was based on the best and worst performance.

Suddenly, I could compete. The standard was not absolute. All I had to do was land somewhere in the range of the other students, and I would be fine. In fact, the natural result of grading on the curve was that students in my class purposefully "dumbed" down so everyone did "well." Nobody wanted to be the one to blow everyone else's test score. *Better,* we thought, *to go forth together in unity and mediocrity.*

Of course, it wasn't always that simple. There were a few despised people in the classroom who actually wanted to set the curve. Every school in America has such a person: The smart, quiet girl with no social life. The nerdy guy who wears starched-collar shirts, corduroy pants and glasses. On test day those few people became public enemy numbers one, two and three. We would pray that certain people didn't show up on test day, because they threatened everyone else's score.

I never was a threat to anyone else academically. One semester I didn't even bother to pick up my textbooks from the school library until the week of final exams. Now that I have grown up a bit, I take a little more pride in my work. When God got hold of my life I underwent a spiritual transformation. Instead of being an average Christian, I wanted to become a sold-out, die-hard curve-setter.

I have found that following the fire is like those tests I took in high school. It presents a threat—the demand that I perform, study, exert some effort.

These times of revival produce curve-setters, people who set a new standard, drive up the average—and may be hated for it. I want to be one of them! The fire of revival separates the curve-setters from the pew-sitters—indeed, it transforms pew-sitters into curve-setters! Suddenly, people who were not part of the church, or were part of the church but blasé about their lifestyles, now want to serve

Jesus around the clock. Their passion burns, their faces glow, their hearts break, their spirits soar. Many times nothing like this has been seen in the church in years, and no one is sure how to handle the flames. Some people sit tight and wait for the fervor of revival to blow over, secretly praying that "average" will be restored soon so they won't have to work harder at their Christian walk.

Don't we know that revival reveals the heart? That it divides people into two groups: people who want to set the curve, and people who want the curve to remain low enough so everybody passes? Pastors and pew-warmers alike can be thrown into conflict when someone bumps up the average as the kids at school used to do.

WHAT IS NORMAL?

Most Christians today hope somewhere in their hearts that God grades on the curve. We want Him to be like the teacher all the students love because she is more concerned that we feel good about our performance than that we score well.

We know that we cannot live up to His standard of perfection—but that doesn't mean we shouldn't try. Don't be content to take what is average and call it *normal*. Some people think that if the very best Christians are living for Jesus about 75 percent of the time, and the worst are living for Him 25 percent of the time, then the average Christian is someone who lives for Jesus 50 percent of the time. Living for Jesus half of the time is something that most of us can achieve. But that is not what God calls *normal*. Paul advised us to go to the next step in our lives by learning to judge ourselves:

> *But if we judged ourselves, we would not come under judgment.*
> —1 Corinthians 11:31

Judging yourself means shooting for the highest goal, not the middle. It's what I'm trying to train myself to do—and what you should do, too. On Judgment Day God will judge us by an absolute standard. He will not take the average test score and dole out our rewards accordingly. The same rules that applied to the apostles Paul and Peter will apply to us.

Many churches have dumbed down these days. I am convinced that what has become average would have been laughed out of the early church. They didn't chafe at meeting more than once a week, at going on long missionary journeys or at giving all their money to help other kingdom workers.

They didn't mind going to jail, being beaten and stoned, being whipped or being tortured. They didn't mind giving up their livelihoods and career dreams—even their families—so they could live worthy of the cause of Christ.

Jesus would never hurry a service because He had something more important to do. He would never be concerned with a service being too loud or too long, and it is hard to imagine Him being offended by someone who showed too much emotion for God.

Jesus showed us an example of a man who was trying to grade his spirituality on the curve in a parable in Luke 18. One day in the temple, a Pharisee stood up and prayed these words:

> *God, I thank you that I am not like*
> *other men—robbers, evildoers, adulterers—*
> *or even like this tax collector. I fast twice a week*
> *and give a tenth of all I get.*
> —LUKE 18:11–12

He was grading himself on the curve. He may have

been an *average* Pharisee, but he certainly failed to understand how to be a *normal* follower of Christ.

In contrast, the tax collector measured himself by true worth and could not even find himself at the bottom of the scale.

> *But the tax collector stood at a distance. He would not even look up to heaven, but beat his breast and said, "God, have mercy on me, a sinner."*
> —LUKE 18:13

He did not look around to find someone worse so he could feel better. His hope was not to receive somehow a higher grade because someone else had a lower grade. His only hope was attached to the words, "God, have mercy on me, a sinner."

The "average" church could handle a little whispered prayer for mercy! But this man's expression of concern was getting a little out of hand—he was not acting "normal" at all. He even beat himself as he spoke. He had stepped out of average and become what *is normal* and right to Jesus. Jesus said:

> *I tell you that this man, rather than the other, went home justified before God. For everyone who exalts himself will be humbled, and he who humbles himself will be exalted.*
> —LUKE 18:14

Are you ready to step out of average and become what is normal and right? Can you imagine the impact you could have on others if you did? How could your church impact your community if it left average far behind and caught the vision of being normal like Jesus?

BLOWING THE CURVE

Revival is when a new generation of curve-setters breaks onto the scene and redefines normal. I so desperately want to be one of them, and I know that you do, too. What does it mean to redefine normal? What is the standard God uses to judge?

To God, a normal Christian is first and foremost sanctified or set apart for God's use only. This is the great battle of modern religion. We all want to be saved, but who wants to be completely set apart? Who wants to blow the curve by being truly holy? It's a hard place to come to.

Average Christianity is defined by living in the valley of decision caught between holiness and worldliness. The average Christian doesn't know whom he wants to serve. He wavers, commits and recommits, then backslides into sin until the next evangelistic campaign.

Curve-setting Christians said good-bye to the valley of decision a long time ago. They made up their minds once and for all. They are sanctified. They are not turning back.

The concept of sanctification confuses some because it is not a word we hear other than in church, but it is explained well by something familiar to all of us—a wedding ceremony. When a couple says, "I do," they vow to be sanctified to each other. They commit to living set apart only for each other. That is the essence of marriage—saying publicly, "I am now given wholly to this person, and I cannot be drawn away."

When a person comes to Jesus and gives away his or her life, it is the same as saying, "I do." Jesus sets that person apart unto Himself. Legally, formally, that person is sanctified and set apart for God's use only. But as with a marriage, nobody really knows if the sanctification will stick until the couple lives it out. There are many storms that come after the "I do."

Having a license and a ring on your finger doesn't make you married in the true spirit of the word. You may still be in the valley of decision although you have vowed to live the married life. In the same way, making a one-time commitment to Christ does not mean being set apart for Him, unless that decision is developed into a lifestyle.

Years ago I attended the wedding of two friends whom I had known for some time. The bride looked beautiful as she walked down the aisle in her white wedding dress. The groom looked stately in his tuxedo, and the wedding ceremony was wonderful. Everyone attending enjoyed the ceremony and anxiously awaited the opportunity to follow them outside the church where we would throw rice at them and watch them drive away to begin their married life together as a married couple.

As they came down the aisle, everyone in the crowd stood up and watched. The bride and groom held hands and beamed, but suddenly the bride stopped before another man whom she had known closely before she met her husband. She put her arms around this man and kissed him on the mouth. Then she and her new husband walked out the back door.

I was absolutely stunned. She had only been married for thirty or forty seconds, and already she was kissing other men! It was an awkward moment for all the guests—and a true-life illustration of how *not* to follow Christ. We can't pledge our love to Jesus and then kiss the world on our way out of the chapel.

SIMON'S REAL PROBLEM

When I think of mixed motives, I think of Simon the sorcerer, whom history has given a raw deal. In Acts 8:13 we read, "Simon himself believed and was baptized. And he followed Philip everywhere, astonished by the great signs and miracles he saw." The Bible gives no hint that he ever performed his magic after his conversion. Yet, he is still called the sorcerer.

How would you like to be called by your former sin even after you believed and were baptized?

Sue, the gossiper . . .

Bob, the enraged husband . . .

Dan, the pilferer . . .

Simon was far from the average Christian. In fact, he appeared to be trying to set the curve. He probably followed the apostles more faithfully than most of the other citizens of Samaria. Yet his famous mistake has defined him.

Simon's legacy in the biblical account reveals that he offered money to Peter and John for the power to impart the Holy Spirit. In reality, his offer was only symptomatic of a great problem, made clear by Peter's shattering verdict: "You have no part or share in this ministry" (v. 21). Why could he have no part or share? Was it because he offered them money? No, money was not the primary issue. Peter identified the problem when he continued, "Because your heart is not right before God" (v. 21).

Having a heart not right before God may come with a variety of symptoms. Simon's was to offer money. But the former sorcerer's real problem was one that is still common today. He thought he could have a part of the ministry of Christ even though his heart was not right before God.

Don't be surprised. That sin is repeated Sunday after Sunday in thousands of churches in America. People think they can teach Sunday school, sing in the choir, preach a sermon, evangelize the lost or serve communion when their heart is not right before God.

Verse 23 makes it even clearer that Simon's real problem had nothing to do with money. The man was "full of bitterness and captive to sin." Countless Christians share these sins with Simon. While we perform our religious acts and duties each week, our hearts are full of anger, unforgiveness, spite and judgment. We are somehow insincere in our service to the Lord.

What if by some miracle the apostle Peter were to appear in a randomly selected church in America? Would he be inclined to treat the people there like Simon? Or even like Ananias and Sapphira, who fell dead under the conviction of the Holy Spirit? I can imagine Peter's words ringing through the modern sanctuary:

You have no part or share in this ministry, because your heart is not right before God. Repent of this wickedness and pray to the Lord…For I see that you are full of bitterness and captive to sin.
—ACTS 8:21–23

Simon asked for prayer, as we all should, but beyond that we don't know what happened to him. There is no evidence that he went back to his magic, but there is also no evidence that he became a long-term follower of Christ. We simply don't know. But we do know that Simon was cut to the heart by truth.

What is your response as the Holy Spirit reveals truth about your heart? Do you go your own way, or do you desperately seek prayer?

When it is revealed that you are following someone else's fire, not God's, what do you do? Ask for prayer or weigh the costs and benefits of each choice?

Being redefined in His image—becoming holy, a curve-setter—is the most wonderful, impacting thing we can do with our lives.

HE MUST BE LORD

Sometimes we can get sidetracked by false teaching that we accept as true. Paul wrote his letter to the Colossians to refute some of the false teaching of his day and to declare that Jesus is Lord of everything. In the first chapter of Colossians he used unusually strong language to describe Jesus.

- ❂ "By him all things were created" (v. 16)

- ❂ "In him all things hold together" (v. 17)

- ❂ "He is the beginning and the firstborn from among the dead, so that in everything he might have the supremacy" (v. 18)

What about some of the false teachings of our day? I once heard a preacher say, "You have made Jesus Savior, but now you need to make Him Lord." Talk about misleading, erroneous teaching! No one can come to Jesus and say, "Save me, but don't rule me."

Some preachers have wrongly divided salvation into two parts—the first requiring mental assent that Jesus is the Son of God, the second requiring that we live under His direction. But they rarely make salvation contingent upon following Him wholeheartedly. That becomes almost an afterthought to getting people simply to say the prayer of salvation.

Given the chance, most people take the easy way out. If they can be saved by mental agreement only, why not quit there? On any given day, polls tell us, more than half the people in America probably say they are Christians and expect to go to heaven. But how many of them are actually living for Christ? One in ten? One in a hundred? One in a thousand? How many will be like the rich man in the parable whose sudden turn of fortune stunned him?

I want to be the one who is found faithful. Jesus is Lord over death and has the power to save, but He must *be* your Lord if you are to escape death. The mark of a true believer is not just being saved from death and damnation; it is the lordship of Jesus Christ evident in that person's life. "In him we live and move and have our being" (Acts 17:28).

JOSHUA'S LAST WORDS

Even people who are experiencing revival can be fooled into thinking that they only need to agree mentally or emotionally with what God is doing in order to be justified. I have seen it happen in recent years. They often think that the presence of signs, wonders and miracles means that God approves of their choices, even if they are not striving for holiness.

It's hard to imagine someone who saw more miracles, signs and wonders than Joshua. He literally followed the fire of God in the wilderness. He had experienced supernatural interventions—the miracles in Egypt, the parting of the Red Sea and the provision of manna in the wilderness. He was there when Moses came down from the mountain with his face shining and when the walls of Jericho came tumbling down. He had witnessed some of the greatest miracles history has ever recorded.

But Joshua did not encourage people to rely on the miracles. Rather, he said:

Now fear the LORD and serve him with all faithfulness. Throw away the gods your forefathers worshiped beyond the River and in Egypt, and serve the LORD.
—JOSHUA 24:14

Repeatedly in his last speech, Joshua called the people of Israel to choose. The twenty-fourth chapter of the Book of Joshua is one of the most rousing parts of the Old Testament and includes this famous declaration:

*But as for me and my household, we will
serve the LORD.*
—JOSHUA 14:15

Sadly, this idea of choosing is all but foreign to many Christians. They somehow think of revival as some mystical power that comes to God's people and overrides their free will. But in the presence of great revival, some Christians still choose the things of the world, the gods of their forefathers, not understanding that no amount of miracles, healings or deliverances will make us more acceptable to God if we are not consistently changing our lives to match His kingdom demands.

Is it possible to go through a great move of God, to witness marvelous miracles and still not believe? Yes.

In the New Testament many people witnessed miracles but did not believe.

*Even after Jesus had done all these
miraculous signs in their presence, they still
would not believe in him.*
—JOHN 12:37

And even those who did believe in Him because of the miracles did not always choose to follow Him. A rich young man received an explicit call to be a disciple of Jesus, but he "went away sad, because he had great wealth" (Matt. 19:22).

What would happen if every church would take the words of Joshua to heart? What would happen if every believer feared the Lord, served Him with all faithfulness and threw away everything that ate up time, energy and money? The answer is clear—we would have nothing short of a world-shaking, humanity-transforming revival!

The signs and wonders we now see in the church would overflow into the public arena. The power of God would become a thing of awe and curiosity to unbelievers, drawing them to Christ.

Of course, that's the way it ought to be already. Revival is not hard to define—it is simply when the people of God begin to serve and obey Him as intended.

When Joshua called the people to choose, they responded, "We too will serve the LORD" (Josh. 24:18). But the old man was wise. He said, "You are not able to serve the LORD" (v. 19). He knew God better than they did, and he knew the people, too. He knew that God is holy and jealous and that the people would not get rid of the foreign objects in their lives. He knew that God's promises were contingent upon their willingness to cast away foreign gods.

You may be familiar and comfortable with many things in your life, but examine yourself—are they foreign to God? Do you have habits, attitudes, a schedule that you would be proud to present to God? The key to having revival, power and a close relationship with a holy God is to get rid of everything that is foreign to Him. God told the Israelites:

Be holy, because I am holy.
—LEVITICUS 11:45

How do we know if we have unholy things in our lives? God often lets us know by withdrawing His presence. He may not bring immediate disaster, but He becomes very hard to find. Prayers seem to thud to the ground like lead. The glory of the Lord departs from us as individuals, and eventually from entire churches if we do not change.

This is probably the most common ailment of "dead" churches today. Religion keeps right on going—even when God is not present. Jesus found the same thing to be true in His day. Religious ritual continued, but the holy of holies was empty.

One of Jesus' goals was to bring the glory of God back to the people of God and the kingdom of God near the people again. How did He do it? He called them to a radical change of lifestyle. He called them to love God with all of their hearts, to forsake all and follow Him.

He called them to be curve-setters.

This is the sign of a true revival of the heart. People set themselves apart for God's use only. That does not mean that a true revival makes everyone perfect and flawless. But it does mean that people repent of trying to obtain the things of God without being holy before God. They make a concerted effort day after day of setting aside everything not of the kingdom, everything foreign to God. What is the result? The presence of God returns in a magnificent, awe-inspiring way to people who thirst for Him.

THE FAİTHFUL SERVANT

For that to happen, we must be faithful servants. Jesus described it this way:

> *Who then is the faithful and wise servant, whom the master has put in charge of the servants in his household to give them their food at the proper time? It will be good for that servant whose master finds him doing so when he returns. I tell you the truth, he will put him in charge of all his possessions. But suppose that servant is wicked and says to himself, "My master is staying away a long time," and he then begins to beat his fellow servants and to eat and drink with drunkards. The master of that servant will come on a day when he does not expect him and at an hour he is not*

*aware of. He will cut him to pieces and assign him
a place with the hypocrites, where there will be
weeping and gnashing of teeth.*
—MATTHEW 24:45–51

How do we be faithful servants? By doing what we are supposed to do until the master returns. Keep in mind that Jesus was talking about a servant, a believer—not an unbeliever. But in the second instance he is acting out of a wicked heart. In the end this servant was cut to pieces and assigned a place with unbelievers. Apparently that is what will happen if a believer has wickedness hidden deep inside.

Many people would be more successful in their spiritual life if they got saved, born again and filled with the Spirit—and then Jesus returned within a couple of weeks. The servant in Matthew 24 surely would not have had a problem if his master had not stayed away for such a long time—but the master did.

If you have ever been married, you know that most couples can handle the honeymoon. There are a few honeymoon disaster stories, but for most couples it's a treasured, positive memory event. It is *time* that becomes the enemy in marriage. The longer you are together, the more hidden stuff bubbles up to the surface that must be dealt with and grown through.

Time can be our worst enemy in spiritual living also. Like the master in Matthew 24, Jesus, our Master, gives us space to stand in His identity and do the work He has assigned us to do. The longer Jesus stays away, the greater the risk of hidden wickedness coming to the surface. With more time, there is more risk of backsliding and turning away from Him.

It happens in churches all the time. A new couple comes, and they look like the perfect addition to the congregation. But the longer they are there, the more their personalities come out, and you begin to see that they carry a lot of baggage from the past with them. Only time will tell if they become healthy, contributing members or if they prove to be troublemakers.

The parable in Matthew 24 says the servant began to beat the other servants and to eat and drink with drunkards. In other words, he was self-indulgent. I imagine this didn't happen in the first week or the first month. But the longer the master is gone, the more time the old nature has to take control.

This is a warning to each of us. We must not leave wickedness tucked away inside. We need to deal with it— and quickly. Otherwise, time will reveal it in the worst way. If you don't get it out, you will have to push it down, hide it and pretend it's not there for the rest of your life. Every once in a while it may rise up, and you may find yourself beating people—maybe not with your fists, but with your words. That's a sign of hidden wickedness.

The intensive, focused times of revival do give people less time to act wickedly. But revival can also lull people into believing that there is less wickedness hidden away than what time would bring to the surface. At some point in the joyful period of revival, people have to purge the dregs of their soul and get the wickedness out. Otherwise revival will be just a temporary covering.

TIME TO RETURN

"Return" is one of the most consistent themes in the Bible. Any church or group of people who return to the Lord with their whole hearts and forsake all other foreign gods, ideas and opinions will find a city-shaking, world-transforming revival of the presence of God in their midst, so that friends and neighbors come to them for prayer and answers to their deepest problems. When we return, God magnifies the result exponentially.

Do you consider yourself saved, but you cannot find God at this moment? Is your connection to God broken, and you don't know how to fix it? Have you wondered what is the root of the problem?

Perhaps we can learn from Joshua, who was still not satisfied when the people declared openly that they would serve the Lord and obey Him. He made a covenant with the people, and he symbolized it by placing a large stone near the holy place of the Lord. He called the stone to be the witness of the people's declaration:

> "See!" he said to all the people. "This stone will be a witness against us. It has heard all the words the Lord has said to us. It will be a witness against you if you are untrue to your God."
> —JOSHUA 24:27

In the same way, Jesus Christ, the living Stone, has heard all that God has ever said to you and every word you have ever said to God. This Stone, Jesus, is a witness to every hymn you have sung, every prayer you have prayed, every sermon, every scripture and every command that you have ever heard.

What does the Stone testify about you?

Does He testify that you waver in your faith, occasionally returning to full devotion, then slipping away again?

Or does He testify that you are a faithful servant, a curve-setter, a follower of fire?

This is your day! The Lord is raising up a new kind of believer who is not trying to cut every corner or live close to the secular edge. They are serious about their covenant with Him and joyfully volunteer to keep their side of the commitment. They want to be holy. They want to be redefined. They are passionate about getting rid of the junky habits or attitudes that cloud their purpose in God. They will not serve the gods of their forefathers or the gods of the people who live around them. They will serve only the living God—they are His soldiers, set apart for God's use only.

Those are the people who experience sustained revival—not just a seven-day high after the evangelist leaves, but a changed lifestyle that is drenched in the presence of God.

They become the leaders of revival. Their lives are more adventurous than a mountain climber's, more thrilling than a high-speed roller coaster, more meaningful than any of the world's philosophies. You can be one of them! You can find your purpose in the fire—and never dream of looking back.

SOLDIERS OF ANOTHER NAME

The presence of God was thick in the place we were meeting, almost as if there were an extra dose of gravity or a blanket laid over each of us. As our worship leader continued in song, I felt the Lord nudge my heart.

"Have the prayer warriors lock arms and march toward the people."

Instantly I had a picture in my head of the Roman army locking their shields together and going forward against the enemy, a perfect picture of unity and strength.

It was the third night of our pastors' conference, and the tent in which we were meeting in Kansas City was packed with pastors and their wives from around the country. The previous two days and nights had been powerful and anointed, and many couples had found new freedom, joy and commitment in their walk with Christ.

It always seemed to take a few days to get to this point. When visitors first came, they were burned out, skeptical and tired. Sometimes their churches had run them ragged, beat them up or dragged them through the mud. Some pastors felt they could no longer hope, love or even feel anything, and others lived in pain because the ministry had not turned out to be what they thought it should be.

But after two days of giving them a safe place to hear about and experience the power of God, most of the pastors and their wives perked up. By the third night of our conference the power of God was flowing with unusual power and freedom. I knew anything could happen.

I stepped up to the microphone and told the prayer warriors of my church to come forward, and then I explained what we were going to do, according to what I had seen in the brief glimpse the Spirit had given me. I knew the result would be a wave of healing sent by God for this very moment and for these very people. The team faced the crowd, locked arms and waited for me to give the word. They looked like a water rescue team that marches into a lake or an ocean to find someone who has drowned—and on a spiritual level that is what they were doing. God wanted to rescue someone, and we were going to serve Him in that effort.

"Go!" I said, and the team took a step forward. An amazing amount of energy was released from them, so much that it was difficult for them to keep moving forward. Several of them groaned, and others could not even speak.

As they continued to walk forward, the people in front of them were hit by the power of God and fell to the floor before anyone touched them. With each step another row of people went down. It wasn't pretty, but people were experiencing instant results. The ushers scurried to remove chairs, and soon people were piled up so high that the team couldn't go any further.

After a while people began to stand up again and praise God, and we immediately asked people who had received from God to come forward and testify.

"The pain is gone," said one woman in tears.

A man showed us his hand that had been withered since a car accident. It was now functioning normally, and his knees were healed, too.

A young man who had been suicidal was released from homosexual tendencies.

It was a life-changing night for many people, and I wondered if the healings would have happened if we had not marched together in unity, like an army, in obedience to what God had shown me. I don't think so. It was a lesson in obedience, but also a picture of what God wants His people to become: a fighting unit that responds to the Commander with singleness of purpose and complete devotion.

SOLDIER VS. CIVILIAN

God calls you and me to be soldiers. This does not apply only to heroes of the faith, but to each person who accepts salvation. We are called to live a soldier's life and, if necessary, to die a soldier's death. Why? Because revival is worth the commitment of a soldier. There is nothing sweeter than the presence of God. It warms the heart, comforts the soul and feeds the spirit—and most of all, it gives us a purpose that will carry on into eternity.

Have you ever considered that your faith might cost you your life? It costs the lives of thousands of people worldwide every year. And many of the people used mightily by God in the Bible, including eleven of the twelve disciples, died for Christ.

Yes, revival is perhaps the most wonderful thing we can experience on this earth, but no soldier goes to the battlefield thinking that his safety is guaranteed. Every soldier, even those who enlist in peacetime, knows there is a chance their commitment will lead to death.

That is one of the major differences between a soldier and a civilian. A civilian doesn't expect to have to give his life in battle. A soldier *must* expect it.

There are other differences, too. Paul said in 2 Timothy 2:4:

> *No one serving as a soldier gets involved in civilian affairs—he wants to please his commanding officer.*

In one statement, Paul defined war's participants. A civilian lives to serve his own needs and desires. A soldier lives to serve the needs and desires of his commander.

The same is true of the Lord's army. There are no civilians during wartime. If a person lives to please himself, he is a soldier of the Lord in name only.

What if a country formed an army and allowed every soldier to set his or her own schedule? No routine, no drills, no training. Just wake up and do what you want. That country would quickly be overcome by an outside antagonist.

The same is true of any church that fails to provide training and discipline for its "soldiers." It will be overcome by the world's problems. Being a weekend warrior in the battle of the ages will bring defeat. It's not enough just to show up on Sunday, shoot a few rounds and claim victory.

Many Christians are so accustomed to civilian life that the soldier's life seems strange and unattractive. They watch the battle from the sidelines—from the pews—but would never dream of joining it. They file out of church after sixty minutes on Sunday morning and consider their duty fulfilled. The "most faithful" are those who show up for the midweek service. These are considered generals and admirals by the people around them, but from God's point of view they may still be privates.

A low level of commitment would get you court-martialed for insubordination if the church were an army. To be an effective army, we have to give our all every day. There is no army reserve in the army of heaven.

A LİFE WİTHOUT OPTİONS

Revival is marvelous because it brings so much freedom to people, but it also narrows our options down to one: Whatever the Lord asks of us. If we are serious about revival, we must face the fact that we have no options. A civilian has thousands of options. Every minute of every day presents an array of choices, but for a soldier the only option is to serve the commander.

Our first example is Jesus. He was the ultimate soldier, and He gave Himself no options. He had every option in the world at His disposal—He could have lived a life of great luxury, fame or political power unmatched in all of history—but He allowed Himself only one option: His destiny. He could have called down ten thousand angels, but He didn't give Himself the option to do it. He said, "Nevertheless not my will, but thine, be done" (Luke 22:42, KJV).

At every step in His ministry, Jesus chose God's option, not His own. When the people wanted to crown Him king, He fled. When Herod wanted Him to do miracle tricks for entertainment, Jesus rebuffed his invitation.

When the soldiers came to arrest Him, He submitted. "I have no other option."

When they hit Him on the face, He stayed the course. "I have no other option."

They spit on Him.

"I have no other option."

They whipped Him.

"I have no other option."

They pressed thorns into His skull.

"I have no other option!"

He stuck to the plan even though He had a body and was tempted in every way humanly possible. He was so compelled by love that He gave Himself no option to live any other way.

One reason Christians fail is because they have given themselves the option to fail. One reason they backslide is because they have given themselves the option to backslide. One reason they get hooked on their old habits is because they give themselves the option of getting hooked again.

They keep the door propped open to other possibilities, just in case this "God thing" doesn't work out.

But options are a soldier's enemy. A soldier would never wake up in the morning and weigh the option of reporting for duty. Yet some Christians wake up each day weighing the option of living for Christ.

Does this describe you? Does it describe someone you know? Do you recognize this pattern in the lifestyles of other Christians? Or are you truly devoted, having ruled out all other options?

I want to be a fully committed soldier, so as best as I can, I have removed all options from my life. Paul compared it to a runner stripping down for a race.

Do you not know that in a race all the runners run, but only one gets the prize? Run in such a way as to get the prize. Everyone who competes in the games goes into strict training. They do it to get a crown that will not last; but we do it to get a

*crown that will last forever. Therefore I do not run
like a man running aimlessly; I do not fight like a
man beating the air. No, I beat my body and make
it my slave so that after I have preached to others,
I myself will not be disqualified for the prize.*
—1 Corinthians 9:24–27

A runner doesn't get halfway through the marathon
and look to the sidelines and say, "I think I'll stop for a
sandwich now." That isn't an option. In the same way,
people in revival shouldn't have options. Church services
shouldn't compete with movies, TV shows or sporting
events, even if they fall on Wednesday or Friday or
Saturday nights. Whatever God is doing, that's where we
should be.

I don't think about doing anything else for a living. I don't
think about what I'll do when I stop preaching. I don't think
about retiring or even taking a day off. The love of Christ
compels me. It pushes me forward. It is my option.

A COMPELLED LİFE

As life changing as this revival has been for thousands of
people, many of us wonder why the world is not turning
to Christ in massive numbers as we want it to. Yet when
worldly-minded people look at Christians—even those
"in revival"—they often see civilians, not soldiers. A soldier is compelled by his cause. A civilian doesn't need to
be compelled by anything but his whims and appetites.

Did you know you can develop an appetite for revival
without developing an appetite for commitment? You can
be in love with the intense worship, the pretty music or
the convicting preaching, but still rebel at giving more
time and more effort to what God is doing. Revival can
become an interesting, passionately held hobby.

In that sense the very best Christians can become much like the very best non-Christians. We might compare ourselves to ourselves, grading ourselves on the Christian curve. But the world compares Christians to themselves and asks, "What's the difference?" Why would an unchurched person join a church with no compelling cause? Who needs another social club?

The key to massive evangelism is a compelled life. Although many Christian television stations run twenty-four hours a day, Christian radio stations are dedicated to Christian music and preaching, and bookstores are filled with Christian books, where are the millions of people breaking down the doors to get in our churches?

They will not come until we stop living for ourselves. Then the masses will take notice. Right now they call us hypocrites. They think Christians are essentially the same as non-Christians, but with a more judgmental attitude and a fistful of rules. In many cases, they are absolutely right. We may go to church. We may pray. We may have some kind of relationship with Jesus. But the bottom line is this: People in the world live for themselves, and many Christians live for themselves. The world is seeing through the subterfuge, and it doesn't want to have anything to do with us.

In 2 Corinthians 5:13–15, Paul says, "If we are out of our mind, it is for the sake of God; if we are in our right mind, it is for you. For Christ's love compels us, because we are convinced that one died for all, and therefore all died. And he died for all, that those who live should no longer live for themselves."

Christ's love should compel us. That's where so many churches and movements are lacking. They build good churches, amazing programs and awesome physical structures, and they even have lively revival services, but the people are not compelled by Christ's love. They are compelled by other motives.

People accused the apostle Paul of being out of his mind because he went beyond what anybody else would do. His reply was, "If we are out of our mind, it's because we are compelled by the love of God."

People have occasionally told me through the years that the people in my church and I are out of our minds. I am glad that we can respond like Paul and say, "If we are out of our minds, it is for His sake. We are compelled by His love to do more."

CHANNEL SURFING

If you are not compelled, then your life will be full of options. Have you ever sat down and started flipping through the channels on the television, and then realized there was nothing on that you wanted to watch? When that happens, you tend to keep flipping around, channel surfing, hoping to land on something compelling.

But there are times when you want to watch a specific program. You turn it to a certain channel and are compelled to keep it there for an hour straight.

In a spiritual sense, most people, saved and unsaved alike, are "channel surfing" for something compelling to hold their attention. When they don't find it, they keep trying other channels—other habits, other religions, other hobbies.

Sometimes churches grab onto revival as the latest trend. If it draws a crowd, they want it. On the surface their meetings may look like everyone else's, but the impact is only an inch deep. How do you tell a lasting move of God from a fad? The people are *committed* and *compelled*.

Christians who hop from church to church are almost always searching for a reason to be compelled. They know that Christ's love should compel them, but they have not seen it demonstrated or lived, so they become wanderers. They go from one church to another looking for someone to model a compelled life, but the preaching they get is more suited to a relaxed commitment.

Their heart yearns for someone to preach a disciplined lifestyle, but they get a heavy dose of noncommittal Christianity under the label of "freedom in Christ." The pastor exhorts them to worship and dance with abandon, but why would they feel like doing that unless there was a real heart change?

To be compelled is to be fixed on one thing. It is to be firm, anchored in divine purpose. It is to have one option and only one.

When we keep our options open, our example becomes useless. Jesus compared it to flavorless salt. We are seen for what we are. But when we are compelled, people take notice. I am reminded of Peter, James and John in the garden with Jesus the night He was betrayed. Jesus specifically told them not to fall asleep, but they fell asleep repeatedly. They kept their sleep option open rather than being compelled to please Him.

If that were the only example they gave us, their lives would have been far from compelling—but we know that they changed. Their love eventually compelled them to die for Christ's sake and to lead thousands of other people to Him.

Many of us have disappointed the Lord by falling asleep during our watch, but the disciples' example gives us hope. *We can change!* We can turn from an *uncompelled life* to a *compelled one*. We can leave our mark on history.

PİLATE'S LİFE OF OPTİONS

Pilate has been portrayed in many plays and television shows to appear as a pro-Christian and anti-Jewish figure. In reality, Pilate was a bad guy, unscrupulous, a torturer who would do anything to make himself look good in the eyes of Rome. He resisted putting Jesus to death, and so history has regarded him as a hero. But he is anything but a hero. And his life teaches us the danger of having options.

Pilate was a great antagonist of the Jews. Every time the chief priests and rulers came to him, he rebuffed them. He did the opposite of what they wanted.

But they finally figured out how to manipulate him. They found the weakness in his character. It's the same weakness in character that the devil finds in you—the desire to embrace Rome, or the world, rather than the invisible kingdom of God. Pilate got caught between what the religious leaders wanted to do with Jesus and what he wanted to do with Jesus. He wanted to let Him go, but they said, "Wait until Caesar hears that you released a man who says He's God over everything."

Suddenly Pilate realized, *This might make me look bad in Rome.* Caught between warring desires within him, he started doing what all civilians do—he weighed his options. Then this one person who had the authority to let Jesus go decided instead that it was better to have Him crucified. Then, to make matters worse, he walked to a pan of water, put his hands in it and said, "I wash my hands of this man."

Pilate wanted to remove himself from the circle of blame. He wanted to make a choice, then act as if he did not choose of his own volition. After all, he did not wake up that morning wanting to come face to face with Jesus. He was forced into a situation that made him squirm, and he tried to have it both ways.

Pilate's situation is really the same one we face today. None of us—not you or me or any other Christian—had a choice about God's bringing revival to America. God did it sovereignly. And we, like Pilate, have a choice. Do we accept the move of God, or do we turn away from it? Do we weigh our options? Do we decide if it's worth it to follow God, or do we seize the opportunity without a second thought?

It's our turn now. There is no washing our hands of the choice. We cannot walk the fence and go along—but only halfway. The Holy Spirit is visiting us and saying, "I'm calling you to live no longer for yourself. I'm calling you to a higher purpose, to the most unimaginable adventures and to a life rich in peace, strength, love and joy."

What are we going to do? The choice is up to each of us. Whether we like it or not, revival is in our hands. We have been invited to follow the fire. You can't wash your hands of being alive at this moment in time. You can't say, "I wish I was living in some other time or place where I didn't know about the move of God."

Through God's glory and goodness and His many precious promises, you can become a participant and not a spectator in the kingdom. He actually offers to share Himself with you! You can participate in His divine nature, see what He sees, feel what He feels, love as He loves and forgive as He forgives. It sounds like a good deal, and it is, but are you sure you want that much of God? It means you will never be able to strike back or return evil for evil. You will never be able to say whatever you want. There are no self-powered people walking in God's divine nature. There are no free agents running around being strong in His mighty power. He shares Himself that He might express Himself through a vessel that has lost itself in Him.

If you and I and every professing believer would enter the kingdom as a soldier, most of the problems of the church would be solved. The fighting among ourselves would stop, the domain of Satan would become completely crushed, evangelism would fly on the wings of eagles and the power of almighty God and the razor-sharp presence of Jesus would ever be with us.

But it will only happen when we stop being self-powered and become God-powered.

WE ARE
NOT SELF-POWERED

God is searching for participants in power who are willing to leave their civilian lives behind. The benefits are plain. The self-powered life ends, and a life powered by His divine nature begins.

Paul tells us to "put on the full armor of God" in Ephesians 6:11, but he first says in verse 10 to "be strong in the Lord and in his mighty power."

We are not called to be self-powered people but to be strong in "his mighty power." If we are not in God's power, we become self-powered people—civilians—possessing merely a cleaner carnality than the rest of the world.

His divine power has given us
everything we need for life and godliness
through our knowledge of him who called us by
his own glory and goodness. Through these he
has given us great and precious promises, so that
through them you may participate in the
divine nature and escape the corruption
in the world caused by evil desires.
—2 PETER 1:3–4

Self-powered godliness will always lead to frustration. The key to a successful Christian walk is refusing to fritter away our lives pursuing other things, hoping we can remain godly along the way. We will be successful when we give our full service.

Yes, being a soldier costs you your life, but it comes with great benefits. An enlisted soldier does not live at his own expense. He has everything provided for him, from guns to boots to food to shelter. As soldiers separated for God's use, we have everything we need for life and godliness.

- Job
- Food
- Clothes
- Home
- Friends
- Purpose

God gives supplies to rookie and veteran alike. No one is led to the battlefield without arms and provisions. The provisions for life and godliness do not come based on past performance, but because of His goodness. You don't have to be the soldier who jumps higher, runs faster or shoots straighter. It is by loyalty, faithfulness and commitment that God provides everything we need.

As long as a soldier is loyal to the cause, the supply continues. You can live for the cause and die for the cause. The only crime is to desert the cause.

THE RIGHT KIND OF WORKERS

When we begin to get compelled by Christ's love, we become the kind of worker God wants in the Last Days. The following well-known verses in Matthew 9 describe these workers:

> Jesus went through all the towns and
> villages, teaching in their synagogues,
> preaching the good news of the kingdom and
> healing every disease and sickness. When he saw
> the crowds, he had compassion on them, because
> they were harassed and helpless, like sheep
> without a shepherd. Then he said to his disciples,
> "The harvest is plentiful but the workers are

few. Ask the Lord of the harvest, therefore,
to send out workers into his harvest field."
—MATTHEW 9:35–38

This passage of Scripture is often used to recruit workers for the church. But this passage is not just about the *number* of workers—it's also about the *kind* of workers. That is clear from what happened immediately after Jesus said those words.

He called his twelve disciples to him and
gave them authority to drive out evil spirits and to
heal every disease and sickness.
—MATTHEW 10:1

Today there are millions of people in full-time ministry for the Lord, but we have very few results for it. The problem is that religious groups are creating workers after their own kind. Each denomination, media ministry or parachurch organization cultivates a type of worker that fits their style.

But Jesus wants workers who are like Him. He is the example. If sheep are going to get a shepherd, then the shepherd has to be God's kind of shepherd—not ours.

What did Jesus do? What kind of shepherd was He? He went through all the towns and villages, teaching in their synagogues, preaching the good news of the kingdom, healing every disease and sickness. That is His kind of work.

Right after talking about the harvest fields, Jesus called His disciples to Him and gave them authority to drive out evil spirits and to heal every disease and sickness. He was giving a demonstration of the kind of workers He wants. If you stop reading the quote at the words "harvest field," you miss the context of the teaching.

To become Jesus' kind of worker takes courage and

revelation. It takes departing from the typical ministry script.

There are many copycat voices in the kingdom today. Many sermons and radio broadcasts are saying the same things we have heard for years. Where are the fresh voices? Are you one of them? Are you the soldier who lives a life without options? Are you the one who moves beyond the wonder of revival to be committed and compelled?

It is so worth it! I wish I could convey the adventures that lie ahead as you move from weekend warrior to full-time soldier. The recruitment office is now open. The choice is in your hands. Let the Lord make a thing of beauty and awe of your life as you serve Him.

FIVE

WHAT GRACE MEANS

There I was, halfway up the television tower in my hometown, with my friend Stan a little ways above me. I don't remember whose idea it was, but we had both agreed on it—we were going to climb the tower. Why? Who knows? Probably because we were adolescent boys with a misguided sense of adventure.

But there I was, the wind blowing through my hair, the sun shining on my face as I hung onto the metal ladder that would take us to the very top. I looked below and saw neighborhoods arrayed in their suburban beauty. I could see their roofs, the backyards, the layout of the streets. The trees looked small, like sprigs of broccoli, and the cars might have been plucked from a toy box.

I looked up and saw Stan, who had paused to look around, too. "Hey, Stan," I said, "keep climbing. Go on up to the top, and I'll meet you there."

"Are you sure?" he said.

"Yeah," I said, half-truthfully. "I'll make it up there in a minute."

I had decided that it would be more fun to hang around where I was and see if I could get Stan to go to the top. Then I would decide whether or not to follow him the rest of the way.

I was enjoying the scenery and wondering how many miles away the horizon was when suddenly, at a much closer location—ten blocks or so—I saw a police car heading toward the tower. I looked up at Stan; he was still climbing. I looked back at the fast-approaching squad car and figured I had just enough time to get down, so I quickly climbed down the ladder. By the time the policeman arrived I was standing on the ground.

The policeman got out of his car.

Poor Stan was stuck. Fear had paralyzed him. He was shaking and afraid to make a move, so rescuers had to climb the tower and bring him down. Our little escapade made the papers, but I walked away from it scot-free. No punishment. No publicity. Just the stigma of having a friend like Stan who was stupid enough to suggest that we climb a television tower.

GRACE TO EMPOWER

As a youngster, that would have summed up my idea of grace: The ability to do something wrong and not reap the consequence.

Many people still define *grace* as God saving us from our wrong choices, but that is forgiveness, not grace. Thank God for forgiveness—I needed it that day at the tower, and most days since—but grace is something different.

The biblical picture of grace is this: *God in action, choosing and empowering a people who don't deserve a thing so that they can be His faithful servants.*

Grace allows people to do what they don't deserve to do. Grace is the power to be what we don't deserve to be and to go where we don't deserve to go—all at God's command.

Instead of being just a truck driver who toils away for a lifetime just to make money and leave a small inheritance, you can be a Spirit-empowered person who prays for people and releases them from demonic bondage. You can have an eternal impact.

Instead of being just a wife, mother and grandmother, you get the added pleasure of being an evangelist who brings many people to Christ.

Instead of being a teenager wasting your life on "self-discovery" or sinful experimentation, you can be a world-changer and impact the lives of thousands of people as a prayer warrior.

God's grace comes in millions of forms, but it always helps us to make a difference for the kingdom.

IS THAT REALLY GRACE?

There is a profound misunderstanding of grace in the church today. Grace is not God's overlooking of sin and wickedness. It is His favor coming to people who don't deserve it. Grace is not to be used as a cover-up for people who bear no fruit, but as the power to do things for God that, as former sinners, we don't deserve to do.

In our society, most people want a gospel with no demands or expectations, and so we use grace as a shield to keep us from sold-out loyalty. A professing Christian who does not want to live like a soldier of God can invoke grace as his ticket out.

But grace is a two-way street. God gives us the opportunity, but we must seize it. We all understand that Jesus set aside the Old Covenant for the New Covenant and that we now live under grace. But do we ever consider what our part of the covenant of grace is? Religion likes to present Jesus' side of the covenant as absolute and our side as open for consideration. We have developed the idea that being saved by grace gives us the right to be a nonparticipant in the kingdom of God.

But a one-sided covenant does not exist. There cannot be a marriage covenant if only one person says, "I do." You can't be a part of a covenant if you don't agree to anything.

How would you like to be married to someone who had the attitude many Christians have? Can you imagine being a wife who cleans, cooks, washes the clothes and takes care of every need while your husband leaves the home for days on end and merely pitches in perhaps on a weekend? What kind of marriage exists if the husband agrees to provide every need, protect in times of danger and pray in times of sickness, while the wife is free to come and go as she pleases without obligation? When the husband complains, the wife says, "I got married under grace; don't put that works stuff on me."

WORKS

Everyone knows that we cannot be saved by works any more than we are married by works. In a way, we all get married in the unmerited favor we have toward each other. Still, a marriage covenant is an obligatory agreement where two people vow their existence to each other. Doesn't the Bible compare the church to a bride and Jesus to a bridegroom? Aren't we living under a New Covenant where we have vowed our lives to each other forever? The Bible does not say, "You now live under grace, so you may do whatever you want."

Many people think that grace did not exist before the ministry of Jesus, as though it was a New Testament invention. They have accepted the idea that the Law came first and then grace. This is not so.

Abraham was chosen by grace. He did not deserve to be chosen and did not earn the right. Israel was chosen by grace. The people of Israel did not earn or deserve God's grace. King David sinned, but he remained king by grace.

Grace has always been God's hand extended to an undeserving people. And the proper response has always been total surrender to what He wants—the opportunity to live for Him.

You cannot earn the right to be married any more than you can earn the right to be saved. But after you are married or saved, the covenant kicks in, and both sides agree to never leave, to be loyal, to be faithful and to serve and love each other forever. It is a marriage covenant. Every other covenant that came before is now null and void.

As Christians, every other agreement we had before Christ is null and void. We leave all and forsake all to follow Him. We have entered into a New Covenant relationship with Christ. It is a two-sided covenant, or it is not a covenant at all. Without question, God's side holds a lot more weight than our side. But our side has requirements.

KEEPING OUR PART OF THE DEAL

We rarely see the power of the New Covenant in our day because while we make God's part absolute, so many want our part of the covenant to be optional. We expect God to provide and protect us while we float along as though unattached. We breech our side of the covenant on a regular basis, all the while holding God accountable to His Word. However, I am convinced that most of the promises of the Bible do not apply to us unless we fulfill our side of the covenant agreement.

God *does* make demands on our lives, and if we don't meet those demands, we suffer the consequences. Jesus said that a tree that does not bear good fruit is only good to be cut down and thrown into the fire (Matt. 3:10). If we lose our saltiness, we are only good to be thrown into the street and trampled on by men (Matt. 5:13).

How can God justify His demands on our lives? Through His grace! Grace has been given to empower an undeserving people. Grace does not remove demands. It increases them.

FREEDOM BY GUILT

Before we can understand grace, we must understand guilt.

I remember sneaking off to the garage of Kathy's and my little house in Smithton, kneeling in the dusty corner and crying out to God to change me because I felt so guilty about who I was. There, amidst the lawn tools and storage boxes, I poured out my heart day after day, hoping that Kathy wouldn't barge in and catch me. I went to the garage instead of the bedroom or bathroom so she would think I was fixing something or just being manly.

But really I was trying to fix my heart, which felt so hopelessly damaged by me . . . by the ministry . . . or, maybe, just by life itself.

For at least a couple of years I did that, wrestling with my own inability to change. Then one day I got tired of the routine. I got tired of trying to convince God and myself that I wasn't so bad after all. That day I knelt in the garage and confessed who I really was, describing my own soiled character in painful detail, then offering myself to Jesus afresh. Suddenly the grace of God flooded my soul, and the truth of grace lit up my mind in a way I had never known.

Yes, I was *guilty,* but I realized that I was not *condemned.*

Like most Americans I had an obsession with guilt. People spend large amounts of money on counseling and therapy to try and get rid of it. Churches have picked up on this and have created a gospel that tries to make us not guilty. The truth is, we are all guilty. Every preacher preaching today is guilty. Every evangelist doing great work for God is guilty.

Billy Graham is guilty.

The apostle Paul was guilty.

Peter was guilty.

Your pastor is guilty.

You are guilty.

And so am I.

We have all sinned and fallen short of God's glory.

Most of us try our hardest to live without guilt. I did for years. I wanted to believe that I had been declared not guilty, but thoughts about my guilt came to my mind even during wonderful times of worship, causing me to feel defeated.

The glory of the gospel is that guilty men and women go free. I am guilty, and I will always be guilty, but in Christ, I will never be condemned. Through the grace of God, this guilty, undeserving man is now able to do and to be and to go because of God's favor.

People will say, "So-and-so makes me feel guilty." But guilt is not a feeling. It is a verdict. You either are guilty, or you are not. It doesn't matter what you feel.

It is time to stop trying not to feel guilty. Accept the guilty verdict, and start enjoying the grace of God. I have found more freedom from acknowledging that I am guilty than I ever found in trying to be innocent. When the devil tells me I am guilty, I agree with him. At the same time, I remind him that he is guilty, too. The only difference is, I have been set free, and he will be locked up forever.

Grace releases us from the verdict and allows "criminals" to become productive workers in God's economy.

GRACE THE TEACHER

Grace is also a teacher. Titus 2:12 says that grace teaches us "to say 'No' to ungodliness and worldly passions."

This is a far cry from a grace that has been used to cover our failures. Instead, it is God in action, teaching us to say no to wrong choices. Many of us never allow grace to get that far in our lives. Instead, we live as immature children who have to be told no so we don't sin.

Parents know a child has matured when he or she can say no to unhealthy things without being told. A teenager who could go to a worldly party but says no has grown up a little more.

Maturity in Jesus is evident when we don't need a preacher or a sermon or even a friend to tell us to say no. By our own choice we say no to every bad attitude, every evil thought and motive. We say no to ourselves when it comes to ungodliness and worldly passions.

When I was a kid, it didn't matter what anybody said; I did what I wanted to do. I didn't take no from anyone, and I didn't tell myself no. If my parents told me not to do something, I did it secretly anyway. It never bothered me that I was disobeying. The only time it bothered me was when I got caught. If I didn't get caught, I slept well.

When I was in the eighth grade, my sister had a brand-new Mustang. That car would sit in the driveway every weekend when my parents went to pick her up from college, and the temptation was too great for me. My brother and a friend of ours would hop in, and I would drive us all over town. Finally, I got caught—not once, but several times—and the police said they were going to throw me in jail. But they never did. It probably would have been better if they had.

I had never been taught how to say no to myself. Now I understand that grace teaches me to say no so God can continue to say yes in my life. *Our "yes" will never work until our "no" gets strong enough.* Let me repeat it: It's no use saying yes to God until we can say no to ourselves.

We may be saying yes to becoming a missionary or

going into full-time ministry. But our ability to say no to ungodliness, anger, unforgiveness and worldly passions may not be strong enough for God to respond.

God is lighting revival fires all over the world. But often, after a short while, the flame dies down to a small flicker because we lack the eagerness for the things of God and cannot say no to our worldly passions, which grind us down. Rather than being redeemed from wickedness, we struggle with it. Rather than being eager to become a purified, set-apart soldier for Christ, we secretly desire the ungodliness that surrounds us.

WHY GRACE WAS GIVEN

Grace is for a specific time in history—the Last Days—and for the purpose of accomplishing God's plan. What we do during the days of grace makes all the difference in the world. Many who think they are "under grace" are squandering God's grace and will face God's wrath.

The Bible gives us a picture of this in the story of the ten virgins. (See Matthew 25.) In order to make this parable fit into our modern theology, some commentators and theologians have missed the true message. It is a story about a day without grace. Caught without oil, five girls could not expect unmerited favor.

In Jesus' day, maidens would dance with the bride and then wait for the bridegroom to be escorted to the bride. The lamps or torches the maidens carried identified the maidens as a part of the wedding party, much the same as driving in traffic with headlights on can identify the cars attending a graveside funeral service. The local police will escort the cars with headlights on through intersections and red lights. Without headlights lit, no one knows your car is a part of the funeral party. In Bible times, as in the story of the ten virgins, if your lamp went out during a wedding ceremony, no one knew you were part of the wedding party.

Five of the maidens were foolish and unprepared and went to buy oil. While they were gone, the bridegroom came, and the door was shut. When the girls returned and begged to get in, it was too late. Their foolish ways had caught up with them. Despite their pleading, the door was not opened, and the bridegroom spoke his chilling words: "I don't know you."

Although some theologians have stated that this parable is about the saved and the unsaved, there is no way that could be so. All ten maidens had lamps and at least some oil and, therefore, had been invited to the wedding celebration. The unsaved will never be invited to the marriage banquet. They would not have lit lamps and would not have even one drop of oil.

The lesson teaches us that even after being called by God, we can be foolish. The time of failure for the maidens came during the time of waiting. God's grace has been given so that during the time of waiting we can all burn brightly. It is during the time of waiting that the foolish are found out.

You cannot call upon grace in every situation. Grace has been given so we can live out our lives in responsibility, expectancy and preparedness. The moral of the story is that we must keep watch and be prepared, because it will be by our lamps that we will be recognized and known.

The best way to understand the parable of the ten virgins is to pair it with the parable of the wicked servant, which can be found in Matthew 24. Verse 48 speaks of a servant who is wicked. Once again, it would be inconsistent with the Gospels to call someone a servant and then say he is unsaved. This man was a servant, but he was wicked. Like the foolish virgins, his failure came during the time of waiting for his master to return. It was then that he began to beat the other servants and eat and drink with drunkards. Like so many in our day, he forgot the reason grace was given, and he became self-serving and indulgent.

Be prepared! Be watchful and careful about how you behave during the time of grace. How easy it is to become lazy, apathetic and self-indulgent, thereby missing the point and purpose of grace.

ANOTHER WEDDING EXAMPLE

In Matthew 22:1–14 Jesus tells a parable about a wedding banquet. Certain people—who probably symbolize the religious Jews of that day—were invited. But they refused to come. The king sent more servants to tell the guests he had invited that everything was ready. But they paid no attention—they had more important things to do. Some of the guests to whom the servants went even mistreated and killed the servants.

Then the master invited more people—symbolizing the Gentiles—and the hall was filled. By evangelical standards, success was complete. What more could we ask for? The "church" was full.

But the story does not end with just filling the hall. While the rest think that all is well, the king notices a guest there without a wedding garment. Something has gone wrong.

The king speaks, calling the man "friend." If the man is a friend, why the terrible ending? The king called him "friend" because he did not know the man's name. It's like asking for directions from a total stranger: "Friend, can you tell me how to get to the church?" *Friend* becomes a generic title for those we don't really know. It's as though the king were saying, "And you call yourself a 'friend,' yet you do not wear the proper garments?" Once again, we hear the theme of "I don't know you" being sounded.

How did he get in dressed like that? Many a preacher has tried to draw conclusions that do not exist. Maybe he forgot his tuxedo. Maybe he was a "party crasher." But with this party, everyone was invited, so no one could crash it. The man was invited, but he was caught unprepared. Like so many today, he worked or played right up to the time of the banquet and was caught with no time to change. Showing up in work or play clothes shows he gave no thought to the invitation—or his need to prepare for the event. He served himself right up to the night of the banquet.

Once the undeserving street people were given the invitation, based on grace, they had to get ready. A grace invitation means stopping life's frivolous activity and accepting grace as time set aside to honor and prepare for God.

In the end, the man was thrown outside, a seemingly cruel postscript to an otherwise comforting story. In Jesus' day, listeners were expected to figure out the moral of the story: He was thrown outside because he had been living outside all along. He got eternally what he had been living temporarily.

Like this man, some today are living unprepared lives, thinking that grace will allow them to go unnoticed. Like the rest of the world, they pay no attention to the days they have been given to separate and commit themselves to Jesus.

Last of all comes the familiar line of that parable, "For many are invited, but few are chosen" (Matt. 22:14). Why are so few chosen? It is because so many live such a foolish lifestyle, hearing the call, but paying no attention. We know the will of God is for us to be commited—heart, soul, mind and strength, but we have many other important things to do. Worst of all, we may squander our lives away in riotous, self-indulgent living.

Grace has been given so we will prepare for the coming King, not so we can feel good about our worldly lifestyles. Grace is for servants—not slackers. Someday the season of grace will end. Then by our lamps we will be known. By our "clothes" we will be judged.

Use this day of grace to get ready, to serve, to set yourself apart. The opportunity will not always be there, so seize it now! Let grace overwhelm your guilt and transform you into a powerful, effective servant of God.

SIX

THE
BATTLE OF REVIVAL

For years I preached and prayed for revival without knowing precisely what it was. I thought it would be a great ingathering of the lost—the town drunks, the rebellious teenagers, the atheists, the college professors, the unsaved masses. I thought revival would be about bringing more people into the church, scrubbing them up and turning them into citizens of the kingdom.

But I would soon learn what revival really is.

I have been to many churches that are having a real visitation from God. It is easy to recognize. The purity, sincerity and commitment of revival lift the spirit.

But I have also been to many churches that say they are in revival, but really aren't. They point to a renewed

The Battle of Revival ❖ **79**

excitement their people have about going to church as evidence of revival. They talk about the long hours they are willing to spend in a Friday night worship service, the freedom they have to praise God with lifted hands and a variety of physical postures and the increased desire to pray for and evangelize the community as proof of revival.

All these things are good, but none demonstrate the heart of revival.

People tell me that revival is an awakening in people's hearts—a special awareness of God. I have experienced that, but it is not the heart of revival. There is more to a move of God than longer, happier services one night a week.

Revival is not a party—it is a war. It comes as an invasion from heaven to shake the foundations of religion, to stir the waters of the soul and to restore honor to the name of the Lord. It is a war in which God sets some apart, sets some on fire and sets some aside.

War brings inner conflict. *Whose side am I really on? What kind of lifestyle do I really want for my family and me?* Some want the God of the universe to host a revival party where everyone is singing and dancing, one where the cries of war are not heard.

In war there are spies, traitors and deserters. Most importantly, God's soldiers can be found. Maybe you are one of them. These brave men and women stand in the wind of His glory and breathe the breath of life from His nostrils. The rookie soldier comes armed with a dream of what real battle is like, but the seasoned soldier knows that dreams alone may get you killed.

Many people are surprised at this characterization of revival. They are taken aback when the Prince of Peace begins to swing His mighty sword to cut, divide and separate His people from all the other people on the face of the earth. We should not be surprised—it's exactly what He said He would do. (See Matthew 10:34.) And when He does, we find ourselves in the midst of a great visitation, one that we are experiencing today.

WHEN REVIVAL CAME

It was difficult preaching about a coming revival to a handful of people in the early years of Smithton Community Church. Revival did not come suddenly as I thought it would. We yearned and prayed and cheered and sang for it, but it did not come. We did not see the evidence of the visitation that we wanted.

Have you ever been in that position? You may want very much for God to visit you, but nothing you do seems to bring Him any closer. I know exactly how it feels, and for me, the pastor, it was especially embarrassing. The empty pews must have looked like fool's gold to any experienced preacher, but I preached as though there were thousands in attendance. I was a small fish in a small pond, and it appeared I would never get out.

From the pulpit I read aloud the astonishing accounts of the Welsh revival. "What would we do if such a thing were to happen here?" I asked. "Would we give ourselves to the work of God?" I remember asking the congregation more than once to imagine people lining up in the morning to get into an evening service. It was a fantastic thought, and we cheered and clapped our hands as if cheering for a dream that had no chance of coming true.

I preached so many sermons in that little church that I could walk forward, backward and up and down the steps with my eyes closed. They were hard, convicting sermons, and people must have thought, *If this guy really knows so much, what is he doing in a place like this?* I wondered that myself virtually every day.

I had turned down a pastoral position at a large church in Chicago in order to revive the closed-down church in

Smithton. I remember so clearly when I knelt in my living room and presented the options to Jesus. I thought for certain that He would point me to Chicago.

"Jesus, what would You do?" I asked, full of self-confidence. "Here is a large church of eight hundred people with a nice salary and all the benefits. Over here is a closed church with no money and no people and apparently no future—in the middle of nowhere. What would You do?"

Without hesitation, the answer came from heaven: "I'll tell you what I would do. I would raise the dead." It was as though the bottom fell out of my heart and landed with a thud on the ground. I was devastated.

Today it sounds almost heroic to say that I turned down a well-paying job in Chicago to go to Smithton. But it was neither heroic nor glorious. Although I was the first choice of the Chicago church, I was the last person Smithton wanted as their pastor! They didn't want a tongue-talking radical in their neighborhood. They didn't want my hard-ball preaching. My music was loud and my sermons long by their standards. I didn't fit their design of a pastor at all. Their hope was that I would come and go as most ministers do in a small town. Neither I nor they realized that God had put down His tent pegs for a long time, and that one day the tiny town would explode with the presence of God and draw thousands from all over the world.

In those early years I was embarrassed to be seen going into the dilapidated building we called church. Kathy and I would sneak in through the back door, our arms loaded with sound equipment. We stuck a sign in the yard that said, "Church tonight." I pounded the piano; Kathy sang with all of her might; and my brother Dan joined in on guitar while an electronic drum machine pounded out the beat. Thirteen people wandered in for our first night, and I began to preach of the coming revival.

Months turned into years, and the old drum machine was replaced with a real drummer, along with many other musicians. Somehow time passed, and we survived like pioneers crossing the dry, desert plains. After a few years most of the services were full, and we started setting up extra chairs on Sunday morning. I had a whole gamut of sermons, from faith to prosperity, but I never gave up on the coming revival.

THE RUMBLE OF REVIVAL

In 1994 Rodney Howard-Browne was holding services in Saint Louis, with large crowds in attendance. I decided to go to see what the meeting was like. There were some things that I didn't understand as I watched the unusual sights and sounds that night. At the time, Rodney's meetings were the closest thing to revival that anyone had seen in recent years. I believed that what I had been waiting to see was beginning to happen. Rodney's meetings weren't crusted over with the same old worn-out religion. They were fresh, exciting and alive. I admit that I wasn't sure that I wanted that kind of revival in my church, but I left those meetings feeling more alive in Christ than I had felt in years. A visitation had started, and I didn't want to miss it.

To stoke the flames in Smithton, we began a prayer meeting on Tuesday nights. It was different from our past prayer meetings, in that the entire church got involved in praying for the glory and presence of God to come in power. Some people even began to "fall under the power" when the Holy Spirit's presence overwhelmed them. It didn't happen to me, but I thought that if it happened from time to time, it was fine. When some of the children began to experience the power by falling to the floor, some of the parents became concerned that they were mimicking the adults. At the time I wasn't sure what was true, but I was sure that we had come a long way from where we had been. The Tuesday night prayer meetings became the best service of the week, and the Lord seemed to be drawing nearer to us.

By March 1996, through a convergence of painful personal events, I was at the lowest point I had ever been. I felt betrayed, abandoned and far from God. It was twelve years since I had started the church, and the revival had not come. I was hurt, deflated, bleeding and hopelessly discouraged. I began to think that God was finished with me.

It was at that time that God chose to visit us. One Sunday evening when I walked into the sanctuary the power of God struck me like a bolt of lightning, and I began to jump up and down. So did everyone else. The chains of emotional and spiritual bondage that had weighed us down were instantly lifted. It was one of the most extraordinary moments of my life, and it kicked off not just a world-changing revival, but a revived lifestyle that we have kept to this day.

WHAT KIND OF VISITATION?

Real revival blew my previous ideas out of the water. Like many people, I thought I knew what I wanted when I prayed for revival. Having seen it up close, I have an entirely different view of what revival is.

In these days of visitation there is more misunderstanding of revival than ever before. Some of the revival myths are so widely accepted that nobody questions them.

MYTH 1: REVIVAL IS INTENDED TO VINDICATE THE MODERN CHRISTIAN LIFESTYLE AND REFORM THE WORLD.

Everybody would agree that when Jesus walked the earth, humanity experienced the greatest revival—or visitation—in world history. And yet many if not most of the people who should have been part of the visitation rejected it. They had a preconceived notion of what a visitation of God was, and they missed it when it really happened. Jesus rode into Jerusalem and wept for it, saying:

If you, even you, had only known on this day what would bring you peace—but now it is hidden from your eyes. The days will come upon you when your enemies will build an embankment against you and encircle you and hem you in on every side. They will dash you to the ground, you and the children within your walls. They will not leave one stone on another, because you did not recognize the time of God's coming to you.
—LUKE 19:42–44

The Jewish people were looking for a time when the covenant God would step down into history and vindicate Himself and His people. That's a strong Jewish theme even today. From the time of the failed revolt in A.D. 6 of a man named Judas the Galilean, to the time the temple was burned and the city taken in A.D. 70, the Jewish people thought God would save them. A remnant fled to the mountaintop called "Masada" and survived for a while under siege from the Romans, but eventually the Romans prevailed and none of those people survived.

Were the Jewish people wrong about God intervening? No. God did intervene, but He did not do what they thought He was going to do. They experienced a visitation that did not fit their expectation.

What was the visitation supposed to do? Exalt the Jewish people in the eyes of the world? That's what they thought, but they were wrong. The visitation was for the purpose of consecration—to set them apart. There would be no liberation without consecration.

These days everybody wants God to come down, clean up the bars, get rid of the crack houses, burn up the abortion clinics and slap the folks in Hollywood around. We want God to show His name strong and vindicate us in the eyes of the world. We want God to show the world how right we've been and how wrong they've been, and as a result many Christians are missing the visitation because they're missing the consecration.

This is not the season to straighten *them* out—it's the season to straighten *us* out.

Jesus came to His own people and said, "The problem is not Rome; the problem is you. Consecrate yourselves to the Lord, and repent of a lifestyle that has no room for God."

Some people are in danger of missing today's visitation because it doesn't look like what they expected. Like the Jewish people of that day, they want liberation without consecration. In churches all over America people are crying out for liberation. They hurt; they need help in their finances, their marriages and their emotional lives. Some people go from church to church looking for somebody to liberate them. They are like the Jews in Jesus' day who thought God would liberate them without consecrating them.

You cannot say, "I want to be free, but I don't want to give my life fully to You." You'll get a little bit free, and then you'll be right back where you were. If you consecrate yourself, then you'll get the liberation. If you set yourself apart to God's use only, then you will have a visitation that will bring liberation.

Trying to make things work without consecration is like a man beating the air. Sometimes we try so hard to make things work. We want the world to turn to Jesus. We want the gospel to pierce people's hearts. We spend millions, and probably billions, of dollars on missions work, television programming, books, tapes, tracts and every conceivable medium to get the Word out.

But the world isn't changing the way we want it to. There are pockets of revival, but they don't seem to affect entire cities or countries. We are like the Jews in Jesus' day. They tried revolts and fighting and all sorts of ways to get victory, but nothing worked.

I read a sign on a church recently that has become fairly common in America. It said, "Join us at 9 A.M. for our contemporary service—come as you are." The only problem is that people are coming as they are—and leaving as they are. There is no change. Churches try so hard to have a celebratory atmosphere, to attract people, to have a good reputation and lively worship. But real celebration is a result of something changing on the inside of a person, not just wearing jeans to church and hearing livelier music. Celebration without liberation is foolishness. It's a religious tactic to get people in the doors. When people realize that it's a heartless celebration, they will go right back to their old lives.

Jesus said that when the prodigal son came home, the father put the robe and ring on him and said, "We have to celebrate because the dead is now alive." That's reason to celebrate.

"I was dead, but now I'm alive."

"I was blind, but now I see."

"I was lost, but now I'm found."

Nothing can take the place of that experience.

MYTH 2: THE PURPOSE OF REVIVAL IS TO INCREASE HEAVEN'S POPULATION.

We tend to think of revival not so much as a time for God to deal with His people, but as a time for God to save more people. Who hasn't attended a service where we were encouraged to bring our friends so they could hear the gospel? Tradition hands us the idea that God's main goal is to keep people out of hell and to get as many people as possible into heaven, and revival is seen as a means to the end. We like the idea of being so important to God that all of His power is being used to get us into heaven.

But it's not true. If God wanted us in heaven so badly, why didn't He create us there in the first place? Surely it must have crossed His mind. After all, heaven is right now filled with all kinds of created beings that will never be seen here on earth. In fact, heavenly angels were intended to be permanent citizens of heaven and were only sent to earth after sin was found in them. Lucifer, filled with pride and rebellion, was flung to the earth with one-third of all the angels. He and his band of terrorists had been roaming the earth long before God created Adam.

Are we to believe that God's number one reason for existing is to get men and women to heaven, and yet He placed mankind, not in the heavenly realms, but smack-dab in the middle of the murderous, lying, rebellious, cut-throat, archenemy Satan's camp?

The myth of a man-centered God is so deeply ingrained that to suggest otherwise comes as a shock. It shocked me when I realized it. But I am convinced it is true: God's purpose for being is not wrapped up in mankind. Rather, mankind's purpose for being is wrapped up in God.

So what is God's purpose, and how does mankind and revival fit into it?

HONOR TO HIS NAME

When Satan rose up against God, justice demanded not just that he be cast down, but that honor be restored. Satan was not merely chased out of heaven—he was followed. God began to dog his every step. He placed mankind on earth, not so we could someday be with Him in heaven, though that is true, but to restore honor to the earth. We are the beneficiaries, but not the purpose of His plan.

God created a man and a woman in His own image. Everywhere the devil looked, he saw something of God. Man and woman were told to subdue and rule the earth. As with any war, there was a great deal of risk, and the new creatures were warned of the possibility of disobedience and death.

But mankind fell into the same trap as one-third of heaven's angels. True to the pattern, the two humans were banished from God's presence. Prevailing evangelical thought tells us that God has spent the intervening six thousand years trying to see how many people He could get saved out of this mess—thus the need for periodic revivals.

But His real goal is as it was in the beginning—to restore order and honor to the kingdom of God. The only way to restore His honor is to have a people committed and faithful to the King—right in the enemy's camp!

Revival is about restoring honor to God, not about populating heaven with more souls. Yes, it is God's will for everyone to be saved, but His goal is to restore honor to the kingdom through salvation, raising up servants who are completely set apart for Him.

I often hear preachers say that the Second Coming of Christ is being delayed by the Father so that more people can be saved. I don't accept this. Where would a loving God draw the line? When is it enough? When are too many in hell? The Second Coming will happen, not when God meets His heavenly quota for human souls, but when honor has been restored to His name in appropriate measure.

Revival was and is heaven's invasion. We are honor-warriors in the enemy's camp. Yes, most of humanity has fallen away from its God and its purpose for being here, but God has a remnant. We are the soldiers who take part in a series of invasions that will continue until the final invasion from heaven comes, with Jesus leading the way and the army of the faithful close behind.

THE CASE
OF EZEKIEL 36

Let me repeat: Revival is not for our sake, but for God's sake. It is about Him, not us. In Ezekiel 36:22 God says, "It is not for your sake, O house of Israel, that I am going to do these things, but for the sake of my holy name." Throughout this chapter in Ezekiel, God tells of all that He is going to do to redeem Israel and bring her back to her own land.

In verse 32, God again says, "I want you to know that I am not doing this for your sake." It becomes clear that God is doing this for the sake of His own great name and honor among the nations. Honor is restored when He shows His name great through His own people.

Even today, we see God accomplishing His goal through an undeserving people. If God can get the job done through the fallen and turn them into the faithful, honor is restored. The focus of the gospel, then, is not about us. It's not even for us or because of us. It is because of His great name, which He will show great among the nations through us.

Most of us are familiar with the parable of the prodigal son. (See Luke 15:11–32.) Typically, we place the emphasis on the lost son and identify with him. But the "lost" son was not really lost. It is very likely that the father knew where to find him. But even if the father sent out a posse to drag the boy home, he would still be lost—because the relationship between the father and son was lost and dead. Since the relationship was lost, finding the son would do no good. The relationship had to be found first.

Why did the father act so graciously to the son? Certainly the son did not deserve such favor. To want your inheritance while your father is still alive is the same as saying, "I wish you were dead." This is the common problem of a man-centered gospel, one that wants what the Father has but cares little about the Father. Many people want to go to heaven because it is the only attractive alternative to burning in hell, not because they want to live with the Father forever. Many are interested greatly in what the Father has, but show little interest in the Father Himself.

The son came to his senses when he wanted to return to his father, not when he wanted out of the pigpen. When the father ran out and threw his arms around the son, the entire community knew that all was forgiven. The father could have run all the way to the pigpen, but honor would not have been restored. The lost son's heart still would have been lost. The son had to return to receive the lavish gifts, showing himself a son again.

But the story did not end there. A second son was just as dishonorable as the first, although he did not realize it. This son, too, was in a lost relationship with his father. The father also had to go after him.

The second son thought "riotous" living was the greatest insult, not recognizing that it was worse to stay and live off his father—and grumble all the while. The second son refused to enter the celebration. The father had to plead with him to have a heart change.

We are not told how the story of the second son ended. Did he repent and join the celebration, or run off and squander his life? Jesus did not intend for us to know, because that part of the story was still being written in the lives of His hearers. *The story of the two lost sons is still being written today in our own lives.*

The lesson of the prodigal son story is this: The religious people who refuse to enter into a right relationship with the Father are more dishonorable than the foolish who come to their senses. Yet, God in His mercy and grace continues to send waves of invasions, often through unlikely people and circumstances, to restore honor to His name in heaven and in the earth.

REVIVAL BRINGS OPPORTUNITY

A real revival brings opportunities that the average person would never have. We see this so clearly in the revival that Jesus brought to Israel. A new opportunity came to fishermen, tax collectors, women, prostitutes and many other ordinary people. Often, those with the most skill, talent and knowledge of God let opportunity pass right by.

The Smithton Outpouring saw ordinary pew-warmers transformed into powerful warriors. In any other day they might have spent their lives twiddling their thumbs and reading *TV Guide*. Instead, they saw the glory of God fall and they stood in its cloud. They watched thousands of lives dramatically transformed and rescued. They prayed for multitudes with amazing results.

Some were educated; most were not. Some lived their lives in expectation, but most were swept away by the presence of God. When their opportunity came, they grabbed it with all of their might and refused to let go. They lived in a continual atmosphere of conviction and repentance. They sacrificed what some might consider a "normal" life. They gave God their best as God gave them the opportunity of a lifetime.

People who follow the fire are desperate for a real move of God that transcends the carefully thought-out programs of "normal" church. Desperate people are ready for God's agenda.

I know for a fact that we were not the only place on the earth that was visited that night. At least two other places with which I am familiar experienced the fire of God, but the people in those churches would not allow the fire to consume their existing programs. At Smithton, everything came to a halt. This was our time. We were determined to grab hold of what God was doing and never let go.

We were determined to overcome every obstacle and every persecution that come with a true move of God.

We were determined to separate ourselves and allow every tradition and preconceived idea to fall to the wayside.

We had no experience with large crowds. We didn't know how to park cars all over town as we do now. We didn't have enough restrooms or drinking fountains or chairs, but we decided to learn.

We didn't know how to usher in the presence of God and keep it resident in our church, but we worked at it.

We were not prepared for the people who would follow me home or wait for hours in my driveway, hoping that I would come out and pray for them. We were unprepared for the threats of violence leveled at me if we did not shut the revival down.

We were determined to learn, to stand and to survive as the fire of God fell in that small, out-of-the-way place in the middle of America.

The outpouring brought death and life to all of us. Many things had to die. We had to die to our own free time and "me" time. We had to die to ourselves and live for Jesus and His kingdom every day. And we loved every minute.

We had found our destiny in the fire.

YOUR REAL DESTINY

Therefore, as we have opportunity, let us
do good to all people, especially to those who
belong to the family of believers.
—GALATIANS 6:10

Our God is the God of opportunity. He opens doors that no man can shut. Revival brings a new opportunity to everyone—including you. What is your response? Do you resemble the people in the Gospels who heeded Christ's call to "follow Me," or do you resemble those who walked away sad?

Nicodemus, though a Pharisee, could have followed Jesus and found his real destiny. The rich young ruler was given the opportunity to become free of the entanglements of his wealth and to lay up treasures in heaven. Even Pilate, with the words "crucify Him" ringing in his ears, could have seized the opportunity of a lifetime to stand up for the King of kings.

Is God offering you a new opportunity? Do you see your destiny in the fire? Is this a time of decision for you? Choose to do some good with your life instead of drifting along with the apathetic crowd. God gave me an opportunity to touch the world from a no-name town in the middle of Missouri, and He can do the same for you, wherever you are and whatever your past is.

But believe me, to advance in this opportunity requires a lot of hard work and faith. When revival came to our church, I had to answer these questions:

⊛ Are you willing to preach five services a week?

⊛ Are you willing to travel to hundreds of other churches?

⊛ What will you do about those who oppose revival?

⊛ What if this move of God only opens you up for more criticism?

Opportunity was knocking, but as I pondered my answers to these questions, I became aware that it would cost me—and my family and church—a lot.

What questions face you in this time of visitation? What could cause you to miss your opportunity? A little entertainment? A few hours of relaxation? A television program? A sporting event?

This is the day of opportunity. The spirit of God is moving and granting us great favor, grace and mercy. Will you lay down your net? Will you walk away from career goals? Financial goals? Will you stand up to the worldly crowd and cry out the message of repentance like a true soldier of the Lord?

You have been called to restore honor to the only One who deserves honor. Revival is upon us; the visitation has begun. Open your heart to it!

PART II

SEVEN

CHANGING DIRECTIONS

Something was different.

I had just returned from a glorious series of meetings in Japan and Singapore. Contrary to what we had been told, the people there were open to revival ministry in every way. The crowds were large, and we were especially thankful for the great number of pastors and leaders in attendance.

But now that Kathy and I and our team were back in Smithton, something felt different. I walked into the church that night for the service, and the atmosphere had changed. It was like coming home to discover that someone had rearranged the furniture. While we were singing and praising, I was keenly aware of what felt like a new canopy that was stretched over us. Something in the heavenlies had been altered, and for the first time I sensed that a major change—even a relocation—might be on the way.

God began speaking to me about moving farther away. There were a number of reasons, some of which gave us great hope. Others were, frankly, heartbreaking.

We consulted with many people, prayed, deliberated and investigated the possibilities. Finally we reached a decision: Kathy, our paid staff and I would relocate the church to Kansas City and continue our revival ministry there.

I began to make preparations to turn Smithton Community Church over to someone else. I approached four different people, but none would take it. Still, I knew that God was moving me to Kansas City, so I went forward with the plans.

When I made the announcement about the relocation to my congregation, I assumed that only the staff and a few other families would go with us. I was shocked when more than 80 percent of the congregation said, "If you go, we go. We are not ready to quit yet."

Suddenly God's plan had grown much bigger. It wasn't just a handful of close associates moving—it was an entire church body. The very idea of moving not just the staff and offices, but an entire congregation, to another city seemed almost impossible. I had never heard of such a thing before.

Kansas City was only two hours away from Smithton, but for most of us it represented another world. Kansas City counted its population in millions, not hundreds. They had an international airport, several universities, big highways, vast suburbs, countless schools and a world-famous downtown section. Everything would be different.

But as we contemplated our move, we knew that not everything would be different. With God leading us, the fire would be the same. In fact, it would burn brighter.

THE PLAN: BUY LAND

The day after the announcement, some people were already looking for new jobs in Kansas City. Not long after that, "For Sale" signs started appearing all over Smithton. Things were moving at a much faster pace than I anticipated or wanted, but I sensed the leading of the Spirit.

People from all over America began calling to find out if the Smithton Outpouring was over. We had to get the word out that the revival was *moving*, not *ending*. We were replanting ourselves, but the services and the visitation would continue.

Where would we move? Our first idea was to buy land along a major interstate where we could build a church. A preacher once said, "God don't make land anymore." In other words, land is valuable to the kingdom. We started scouting properties. I drove down the interstate, craning my neck to see what each parcel of property looked like.

Being from the country, I didn't realize that land along an interstate near a major city could cost a fortune! I inquired about one piece of property that looked perfect and was shocked when they said, "That land is a good deal; *only ten million dollars for five acres.*" That kind of "city" sticker price blew my "country" expectations out the window.

I am not one to limit God, but that kind of money for land alone—not to mention the buildings we would have to construct—was more than I could swallow. I was full of faith, but my faith said there was a better deal somewhere else. We began to look for an existing building to give us an intermediate step.

The move gained more momentum when a church in Kansas City offered to lease their old church to us for more than two years with an option to buy. They said we could start almost immediately. The sanctuary seated nearly twelve hundred people, and there were also wonderful classrooms available. As I toured the campus I even dreamed of starting a Bible college.

We signed a contract with the church for a twenty-seven-month lease, and everybody started moving. We were following the fire, even if we took a temporary, unexpected detour.

AN EASY REVIVAL

Revival is easy when it means coming to church and being blessed by God. But it's hard when it means leaving your home, your normal schedule, your plans and working hard to keep the revival going.

It's easy when you feel the showers of blessings on your face during worship time. But it's hard when searing hot air from the Refiner's fire blows over you.

It's easy when you know where you're going. It's hard when you have to keep going by faith, not knowing where each step will take you.

Abraham is one of the best examples in the Bible of a man whose life went through the stages of revival. The more I think about his life, the more I understand why he was called the father of faith. It was because he kept going when it would have been easier simply to stop.

When God gave Abraham a promise, it was very specific: "I am going to give you a son, and you will be the father of many nations." We can spiritualize that, but it actually meant that Abraham would bear a physical son and that a nation of people would spring from him. It did not mean simply that Abraham would be remembered by many people as the father of faith, although that is true. It meant he would receive an actual, tangible promise: a baby boy.

It probably would have been easier to believe God for

the long-term, spiritualized promise rather than the short-term, physical promise of a son. The spiritual promise held no risk: Abraham would not be alive for its fulfillment, so he could believe it without being disappointed.

But to have a son in his old age—that was a tougher sell. It required Abraham to believe for a real-time, see-it-with-your-own-eyes miracle.

Today there is a lot of prophecy and preaching about a great worldwide revival. I have been in many meetings where preachers talked about revival coming to the world, and I've seen people applauding heartily at the promise of revival. Many people talk about revival coming to specific foreign countries such as China or India—and about revival in America.

Those statements may sound wonderful—and they are—but they do not represent the kind of faith Abraham had. Abraham's faith was specific and personal. He had faith for a certain type of miracle in his own life—not someone else's life or someone else's city. His faith operated where he lived.

It is easy for you and me to believe for revival in China, but it is much harder to believe for revival in our own church or life. We applaud the declaration of world revival, but we often shrink from the promise of revival in our family.

To really have Abraham's faith we have to say, "God is going to send revival here, not just over there. He's going to bring life to our dead marriage, ministry or church just as He brought a son out of Abraham and Sarah's bodies, which were as good as dead."

BELIEVING AFTER THE PROMISE

Abraham's faith didn't stop there. Isaac was indeed born, the promise was fulfilled, and Abraham surely must have thought he had crossed the finish line in the marathon of faith. I could have reached the place where I felt like congratulating myself by saying, "I've done it. I won the battle. I stood the test. I believed God, and now I can relax."

But it was at that point in my life when the bigger test of faith began.

God told Abraham to take the son of the promise and sacrifice him. We all know the story, but I am not sure we understand it in light of today's revival.

Revival is like a promise God brings to churches and people who are, like Abraham's body, as good as dead. Somehow, by faith, we hold on to the promise through years of heartache and disappointment, and finally it comes to pass. The church is revived, sin is held at bay, holiness reigns, and love for Jesus is at an all-time high. That is where most people think revival ends. We see a finish line; however, God sees a starting line.

The test of faith does not end with revival. Sometimes we believe for revival for so long that when it comes, we feel like letting down our guard and shrugging off the great faith that got us to that point. But Abraham's example tells us to go further.

Abraham believed God after the very promise he had received was threatened. When your life or ministry faces opposition or transition, that's when the test comes. That's when God says to march up the hill and give up your son.

That is the kind of trial I felt we faced moving to Kansas City, and I know you have faced similar trials. It is tempting to want to stick with the old, familiar ways, but we knew God had told us to move from Smithton. For me, it was like giving up a son. I asked God, "Do You want me to take my 'son,' this revival, and kill it? Walk it up the mountain not knowing what will happen when we get there?" I had to take it to the mountain and let it die, and as a result, God gave us something better than we had.

I travel all over the world to places that are hungry for revival, or to places that have experienced the beginnings of a revival and want more. It's wonderful that I get to be with them, and the ministry is usually very effective. But my team and I only get results when a congregation doesn't try to make me their "Abraham." If a church is to have revival, the pastor of that church has to be the Abraham in that situation. Every person in the church has to be an Abraham. Each person must decide that revival life and miracles will come through him or her—and will keep coming even when the move of God hits a snag, a wall or a sand trap. No preacher is good enough… no authority strong enough… no anointing powerful enough to override people who are satisfied with the status quo and stop when faith says, "Go on."

BAD NEWS

"What have I done?"

I mouthed the words as I sat in the empty little house adjacent to the church back in Smithton. My voice was weak, my heart wounded. I looked around. Nothing was left on the walls in the kitchen or in the living room. The family that once lived there was gone and had left nothing behind but silence. The dripping of the faucet sounded like small cannon fire as it echoed across the bare linoleum floors.

There were other houses like this one in Smithton— bare, waiting for their next occupants. It was only a matter of weeks since I had signed the lease with the church in Kansas City, and already many people were moving out of town in anticipation of starting our services there.

The thought came to me again.

What have I done?

No one answered. The silence was eerie, and the house became my closet with God. Its bare walls made it a wilderness experience. There was no place for my eyes to rest, no photograph, no work of art. I sat in the middle of the floor and thought back to the hustle and the bustle of the last three years.

That hustle and bustle might never be seen in Smithton again. No longer would hundreds of people stroll along Clay and Chestnut Streets where the church sat. In three years, it was estimated that nearly a quarter of a million people had attended our services. Now the parking lot was empty. There would be no more laughter and singing in the streets. No car doors slamming like drumbeats at one in the morning. There were no more angry neighbors trying to sleep as horns honked and people waved good-bye.

The fire had moved, and we were following. But I was learning that following the fire is not always easy. In fact, sometimes it is very costly.

As I sat in that empty house in Smithton, I held in my hand the useless contract. I had just heard the news that the building we expected to occupy in Kansas City would be sold. The church board had been expected simply to rubber-stamp the committee's recommendation of our contract. However, one man filibustered, delaying the vote, and the church decided not to bring the contract up for consideration again. It was void. And we were without a church home.

All that planning . . .

All that moving . . .

All that praying . . .

Now what? No place to meet and no clear idea what to do. Silently I inquired of the Lord, "Have I been wrong all along, or is this just another hurdle?"

We had followed all the steps to revival about which I have already talked in this book:

- We followed the fire of God, leaving behind the pattern of church life with which we were comfortable, letting God define our relationship with Him.

- We did our best to lose our old identities and to find our identities in Christ.

- We lived the lives of soldiers, set apart for God, with no other options but His work to engage us.

- We seized the grace we had been given.

- We recognized the visitation God had brought and endeavored to consecrate ourselves.

It seemed to me that we had done all the right things. We were still having services twice a week, and God's power was evident in every meeting. We were still fielding dozens of phone calls every day from around the country.

But now there was nothing to say. The hard work of the last few months added up to nothing. No building . . . no land . . . no place to go. How was I to tell the congregation? What would I say to the reporters, the ministers, the revival-hungry Christians who called?

The fire of God does not always give us full knowledge. Anyone who follows the fire can attest to that. As I held that worthless contract in my hand and asked God how He was going to straighten out our situation, I had no idea how He would respond. From my point of view, we were a church without a building, a people who had sacrificed everything to move to a new place. Now our plans had hit a serious snag.

Everyone had been so sure that the building in Kansas City was the one for us; I dreaded the thought of making the announcement. I was concerned that people would doubt that we had heard from God. I thought about the few who had stayed behind and opposed the move to Kansas City. Probably they were having a laughing party, toasting the church's demise. Perhaps they thought I had gotten too big for my britches and was now paying the price.

DON'T GO BACK TO EGYPT

That was when the temptation began. There we were, a church caught between two cities. We had declared Kansas City to be our new home, but the only building we owned was back in Smithton. It now sat empty and mostly unused. Most of the people had already relocated to Kansas City and were driving back to Smithton for services, but that kind of schedule couldn't last long. I felt we were losing momentum fast. Suddenly we were in a wilderness I had not anticipated.

A lot of people advised me to go back to Smithton and stay there until we secured a building in the city. I knew we couldn't do that. It wasn't about location, and it wasn't about me being stubborn. It was about honoring God.

One of the reasons we had moved from Smithton was the incredible opposition the town had brought against us. The spiritual climate there was as toxic as any place I have known (which is why none of the people I asked to take the church would do it). People would literally yell and curse at us when we walked by, and we felt physically in danger. The tension between the Spirit of God and the antichrist spirit became intense, and God finally said, "Escape. Don't stay here any longer."

We knew what it was to stand and fight. But God was telling us to move on. To make it worse, I reflected back on the small group of people from within the church who had grumbled against God before we decided to move, and whose words actually changed the heart of God. They said things like, "I wish we had our old church back."

That may not seem like much of a statement, but consider that thousands of people around the world were praying for exactly a revival like the one with which we were already blessed. It was as though these grumblers were standing at the pillar of fire and saying, "Let's go back to Egypt." That kind of thinking didn't set well with God when the nation of Israel did it, and it wasn't pleasing to Him in Smithton.

To go back to Smithton—the place where God had been dishonored—would have been wrong. Yet I knew that we could conceivably go back and continue the revival as it had been before, even though it would probably plateau. I thought about Moses striking the rock to produce water for the nation of Israel. That worked the first time, but when he did it the second time it went against God's new plan.

When we needed water the first time, God struck in Smithton. But when we needed it the second time, it would not be right to strike the rock again. It was about obedience, not about doing what we knew would work.

There we were in limbo. I felt as if we had come out of Egypt only to find ourselves facing the Red Sea. We had nowhere to go but back. But going back was not an option. We chose to press on, without a place to meet, without clear direction—just one step of faith at a time.

OUR REAL STRUGGLE

When we were stuck without a building for months, God dealt with many of us about our faith levels. Were we willing to keep going forward? Was the promised land worth it? Did the enemies appear too large, too threatening? Did we feel like grasshoppers in their sight?

Revival is, among many other things, a sifting device for the spirit. It exposes motives you and I would rather keep hidden.

If you have been a Christian for even a short amount of

time, you know what these kinds of wandering experiences are like. The lush landscape that once surrounded you gives way to dusty desert. Abundance gives way to the bare essentials. You pass from a time of rejoicing to a time of hunkering down and praying for deliverance. It is a time of struggle.

Many, and probably most, revivals stop when struggle begins. I am reminded of the believers to whom the Book of Hebrews was written. They were Jewish Christians who were facing persecution. They weren't being martyred, but they were under a great deal of pressure. What Jesus had done in their lives was becoming unpopular, and suddenly they had a choice to stick out the commitment or shrink back. That's why the writer said to "fix your thoughts on Jesus" (Heb. 3:1). There were a lot of other things those early believers could think about besides Jesus—but only He could bring revival in the face of persecution.

The Book of Hebrews could have been written to the church today. It tells us to stick with the commitments we've made, to press on in the face of difficulty. What's happening in our lives is what was happening to the Hebrews.

I find that many people who go to church, and even many people experiencing revival, are not in spiritual warfare with the devil as much as they are in a struggle with God. The Bible says that our struggle is not with flesh and blood, but with principalities and powers in the spiritual realm (Eph. 6:12). But most people are not fighting at that level because they haven't graduated from struggling with God. Christians love to sing about the devil being under their feet, but most people have not really faced him yet. Like Jacob, they are still wrestling with God, deciding how far they will go in their faith and how much they are willing to be changed.

God's goal with you is what it was with Abraham: He wants to make you into something that you're not sure you want to be. When I pray for people, I can see their hearts breaking because inside is a call, an appointment with destiny, but they have never been able to break loose of the criticism they face for the unpopular stance God wants them to take.

The call to preach came on my life when I was six years old, but I backed away from it and never considered it again until I was twenty-three. When I faced it, I faced it with courage and made a long-term decision to embrace that call. I have been preaching ever since.

Within your heart, God has placed a commitment to Jesus that may be greater than the level of commitment in which you are now living. In seasons of revival many people step out of their former lifestyles and begin to live up to their commitments. When they do, the temptation and criticism intensifies—people want the "old you" back; you want to do what you used to do with your free time; you want to have a little more say in your life; and eventually you may abandon God's call.

You probably wouldn't abandon Jesus totally. Most of us don't. But we do abandon the level of Christianity in which we were called to walk. We want to "tiptoe through the tulips," but we were called to be people who walk through the fire and are not burned.

The writer of Hebrews told his readers to be careful not to fall into the same sin of unbelief. That is a warning that should be well heeded today. He did not mean unbelief in Jesus. He meant a state of living below the call of God. As an example, he used the time when the Israelites were given the opportunity to enter the Promised Land, but the majority of them failed because they lost their courage through unbelief. They were still God's chosen people, but they suffered the consequences for unbelief. They fell well short of the call on their lives.

Today God is calling for believers who will live with

Abraham's faith. These people are aware that the land in which they live desires to devour the faithful. They know that anyone who follows the fire of revival will face temptations and challenges, but these faithful soldiers are not willing to back away.

When you face a trial or an insurmountable wall, do as Abraham did—obey and keep walking. Don't let revival fizzle out in the face of trouble. Fight for it. Seize it afresh. Don't let the visitation end. God will certainly provide a way to overcome.

Our experience in this season of transition taught us many important lessons about how to stay in the path of revival—even when the pillar of fire is moving in a new direction. If we had failed to learn these lessons, we would have been unprepared for the next step of God's plan. You will no doubt also have an opportunity to learn these lessons. They included the following:

- ❀ Expect God to change the direction of His fire from time to time.

- ❀ When God tells you to move, be sure you follow His direction in determining your new location.

- ❀ When the refiner's fire blows over you, keep going by faith.

- ❀ Believe for a real-time, believe-it-with-your-own-eyes miracle.

- ❀ Trust God for revival right where you are.

- ❀ When revival comes—get prepared for the next test right behind it.

- ❀ Never turn around and head back to "Egypt"!

- ❀ Don't fear the wilderness—keep your eyes on the pillar of fire.

❀ When the going gets tough, don't abandon your call—get going to your promised land.

❀ Do as Abraham did—obey and keep walking.

When you have faithfully learned these lessons, watch with expectancy for what God is going to do to burn your fires of revival brighter than they have ever burned before.

EIGHT

COVER THE CITY IN GLORY

L osing the lease on the church facility in Kansas City was followed by an even more disappointing fiasco that involved a department store building at the intersection of two major highways. A large store, formerly housing a K-Mart, stood empty, and K-Mart was willing to sublease the space. The location was perfect, and it would have given us just the visibility we wanted. The building was huge and empty—waiting, we thought, for a revival church like us to move in.

For several months we put all our effort into preparing to move there. I visualized holding pastor's conferences there. I imagined what worship would sound like in that large space and how we would conduct the prayer times. It seemed that we had a green light to lease the place—nothing stood in our way. Finally, we were going to get a building.

But on the day before we moved in, we discovered that K-Mart did not have the right to sublease the building to a not-for-profit corporation. Suddenly a huge brick wall shot up right in the path before us.

I was disheartened by the news and kept thinking, *This revival IS of God, but why do our plans for a new building keep falling through?*

Amazingly, the families who had moved with us never doubted. They dug in, kept buying and selling houses even though I had to tell them I didn't know where we would be meeting. Once again we were without a building. We didn't even have the prospect of a building. If the situation hadn't been so close to my heart, I might have found it comical.

WHAT NEXT?

I had one of those extended, internal conversations with God. It continued for some time. In the meantime, the phones kept ringing. Each time I had to explain that, yes, the revival was going strong—we just didn't have a place to meet.

On the night that I heard the news from K-Mart, I went deep into prayer. While praying, a phrase popped into my heart. Soon it began to sound like a drumbeat: "Cover the city in glory." It had to be God's idea because I didn't know what it meant. How was I to "cover the city in glory" when we had no place to meet? It occurred to me to rent a hotel or meeting place on a weekly basis, but none of the places available had every week open. And I knew that a temporary setting like that was not an ideal situation anyway, because it did not encourage lasting change. Yes, lives were touched, but the local congregations never really changed. Those who attended these temporary, come-and-see-what-God-is-doing kind of meetings seemed to calmly return to their own churches, where business went on as usual.

Lord, how do I cover the city in glory?

I was willing, but I didn't know the answer. Each night I slept only a few hours, and then I wakened with the phrase bobbing to the surface of my soul: *Cover the city in glory.* On those long, sleepless nights, I began to think of all the churches in the greater Kansas City area that were never used on Friday and Saturday nights. Then I remembered all the churches that had been supportive of the Smithton revival before we decided to move.

Slowly the thought emerged from the depths of my soul: *What if we went to local churches, taking our entire congregation, sound system, worship team and all, and held revival services there?* It would be as if we were taking a tour of churches in the Kansas City area. Now I felt that I was making progress. We could influence the spiritual climate of the city, bless other congregations and keep the flames of revival going. I took out a map, drew a circle around the city and marked the churches that had supported our revival. They were not large or influential, but I knew they were hungry for a move of God, and that was good enough for me.

I talked with our staff and pastors. They liked the idea, but raised a good question: Would these churches want to turn over their entire church to us? How would they feel about being overrun by another congregation?

We came up with an answer: What if we held services on Fridays and Saturdays, but on Sunday mornings, we became their congregation? We would support and encourage what they were doing as a way of recognizing and validating their ministry. They could do all of the praise and worship and preaching, and we would add the "amen" to everything. And we could give into their offerings.

My congregation loved the idea, and so did every church we contacted. They wanted us to bring the outpouring to their neighborhoods. Within a few days the schedule was set. We would go to each church for two weeks and then move across town to the next one.

Suddenly the adventure was back!

WHY ARE YOU SO AFRAID?

Never have I felt more like a living biblical portrait than during those wilderness months. Not only were we a people who just left Egypt (Smithton), but now we were wandering in the desert like the children of Israel.

Were we excited? Yes.

Was there a sense of anticipation? Yes.

Were we afraid? In a way, yes. We did not live in fear, but the option was always there to let fear take over. We did our best to resist it.

I knew that facing trying circumstances was a part of living the Christian life. The Bible bursts with examples of people being forced into frightening situations that test their faith. In Matthew 8, Jesus and the disciples headed onto the lake just in time for a storm.

> Then he got into the boat and his disciples followed him. Without warning, a furious storm came up on the lake, so that the waves swept over the boat. But Jesus was sleeping. The disciples went and woke him, saying, "Lord, save us! We're going to drown!" He replied, "You of little faith, why are you so afraid?" Then he got up and rebuked the winds and the waves, and it was completely calm. The men were amazed and asked,

"What kind of man is this? Even the wind and the waves obey him!"
—Matthew 8:23–27

The disciples had reason to be astonished. At least a few of them were experienced fishermen and had probably seen boats sink before. I am sure they had even lived through their own share of storms, and each one of them probably had a couple of harrowing experiences under his belt.

In other words, they had more experience with storms than with God, and that experience was the basis for their fear.

Some of us have more experience with storms than we have with the power of God. Like the disciples, we can flow in the power of revival until a storm hits, then suddenly we revert back to our prerevival mentality. Past experience starts to shout down our faith.

During our time of wandering and covering the city in glory, God asked me that same question over and over: "Why are you so afraid? Sure, you're in a storm, but you're on your way some place. God's up to something. You're going to make it because there's something for you to do on the other side."

Those words of comfort meant everything to me. Nobody wants to wander without purpose. If you have to go into the desert, you want to know that something is waiting at the end of the journey. If you are forced to ride a boat into a storm, you want to know there will be fruitful ministry on the opposite shore.

LEAVİNG THE PAST BEHİND

When the rain and wind started pelting the boat, I can imagine the spreading tension that overtook them. Pulses quickened. Knuckles gripped the planks as the boat rocked more and more treacherously. I can imagine the quick glances at land to see if they could swim to safety.

I picture the once glassy surface of the lake heaving water upward in rising and falling pyramids, and the boat being thrown from one wave to the other, sometimes landing, jarringly, in the trough. I can almost hear the sounds changing—from the gentle lapping of water at the boat's bow to the hard slap-and-whoosh of waves buffeting the boat. I can see water sloshing into the hull and pooling in the lowest part. I can hear the tone change among the dozen men from casual conversation to nervous observation about the weather to barked commands meant to keep the boat from going under.

What is harder for me to picture is Jesus sleeping through the ruckus. Growing up near Galilee, He too must have heard firsthand stories of boats sinking in sudden squalls. Yet there He was, sawing logs while the boat pitched and rocked. It's one thing to sit calmly and watch or to help bail out the water and maintain a sense of calm. But sleeping?

It took the stormy time in my own life to understand why Jesus could rest and what that means for us. Yes, as all our Sunday school lessons teach us, we are safe when Jesus is in the boat with us—or rather, when we are in the boat with Jesus. That is the most basic lesson. But there is more to the story, and it involves the unique time and purpose the disciples were living in.

This wasn't just a boat full of men. It was a boat full of men living in the purpose of God. They had a destiny and a calling to fulfill the will of God in their generation, and that meant getting to the other shore where Jesus would deliver two demonized men and turn them into evangelists. Were they protected because God loved them more than other Jewish believers? No. They were protected because God had chosen them to participate in a time of His visitation.

When we live in a time of visitation, as we are today,

there will still be storms. But for those people who follow hard after God there is special protection. It's not because God prefers us but because we have said yes to His plan.

The other big lesson is that we must let the future set our faith level, not the past. The disciples let their past experiences dictate their faith levels—or in this case, their fear levels. Had they seen the ministry that awaited them on the opposite shore, they wouldn't have worried. Instead, their minds were crowded with memories.

Remember the last time this happened? We almost drowned.

Some fishermen I knew a few years back were caught in a storm like this, and they never came back.

Everyone knows there's no way to survive these things.

Though they had been living with the very Son of God and experiencing miracles beyond comprehension, they snapped back to the mind-set they had before they ever laid eyes on Jesus. Not only did they discount their future ministry—they seemed to forget the recent ministry as well.

In the time of God's visitation, all past experiences with storms are invalid. They don't apply. They don't fit into what God will do. You can't predict God's future plan based on past storms.

If only we could sleep through storms as Jesus did! He wasn't being arrogant or conspicuous as He napped in the boat. He was simply acting on the fact that fear was invalid. He recognized that no storm could thwart God's time of visitation. He didn't look backward for an explanation—He looked forward.

I believe that is a word of encouragement for every person who has embraced or will embrace the move of God. Why are you so afraid? Don't you understand that God is up to something, and you're right in the middle of it? No storm can touch you when the Savior is in the bow of the boat.

It is time to stop living backward, framing each new thing that happens in reference to the past. We are in the middle of one of God's great revivals, and there is much more to come. That is the context for your life, not the storm you are facing. Set your faith on the future, not the past.

DON'T WAİT FOR THE MİRACLE

We cannot wait for a sign from God to activate our faith. Before Jesus rebuked the storm, He rebuked the disciples.

> *He replied, "You of little faith, why are you so afraid?" Then he got up and rebuked the winds and the waves, and it was completely calm.*
> —MATTHEW 8:26

Why did He deal with the disciples first? Because their fear changed the way God wanted to handle the storm. If they had been full of faith, Jesus would not have had to do anything. He could have rested.

Jesus is calling us to believe without a sign that He is on the scene. He is calling for us to get the context right without having to see a miracle. Most of the time the storms of life should not require a dramatic sign, just calm faith. Instead of saying, "God, take away this storm!", we should speak to ourselves and remind our own hearts of His promise for protection. We should say, "I am part of God's plan, working for His purposes, and I know there is ministry He wants to perform on the other side of this storm. Therefore, I will not be afraid. Nothing can harm me until His purpose in my life is fulfilled."

That may not calm the storm on the outside, but it will calm the one on the inside—and that's the one that really matters.

One of my favorite scriptures says:

God is our refuge and strength, an ever-present help in trouble. Therefore we will not fear, though the earth give way and the mountains fall into the heart of the sea, though its waters roar and foam and the mountains quake with their surging.
—PSALM 46:1–2

At the very end of the chapter in verse 11, the psalmist says:

The LORD Almighty is with us; the God of Jacob is our fortress.

This is a reminding psalm. It is not a prayer to be delivered from the storm, but an affirmation of what is really true about the situation. God didn't say to deny the circumstances—He instructed us to interpret the circumstances differently. Nowhere in the Bible do you find teaching that says, "The storm doesn't really exist. It's all in your head. Just imagine it differently and it will go away." God is realistic and practical. Yes, mountains were falling into the sea. Yes, the waters were roaring and foaming, and that could be scary, but the reality was, "God is our fortress, an ever-present help in trouble."

That is called *seeing with eyes of faith.* One of the best ways to exercise those eyes is by putting the right things into your ears. Paul wrote:

Consequently, faith comes from hearing the message, and the message is heard through the word of Christ.
—ROMANS 10:17

One summer night when I was a boy, I went to see a horror movie called *The Birds*. It ended at around 8:30 P.M. when dusk was falling. After watching the birds in that movie take over a town and terrorize people, I walked out of the theater and into the twilight, knowing I had to walk from downtown to my home, which was a pretty long distance. To make it worse, there were huge trees all along the way, and they were full of birds coming to roost for the night. Those birds had never bothered me before, but because of the movie I thought they might change their ways and come after me.

It was a long, scary walk home!

I learned then that not only does faith come by hearing, but fear does also. That movie had pumped fear into me, and I started living afraid.

The world is filled with fear-inducing messages. Everything from newspaper headlines to conversations at work to songs on the radio can cause a fear response to rise up inside us. Sometimes all you have to do is look at your bank account to feel as though you've just watched a horror movie!

Those sources of fear must be countered with sources of faith. Imagine what would happen if you surrounded yourself with fearless people. Jesus exhibited faith's fearlessness in the boat. Peter demonstrated it on the Day of Pentecost when three thousand were saved. It filled the heart of Stephen when he testified for Christ, and fearlessness shone on his face as he was stoned to death. As Paul sat in a Roman prison awaiting execution, fearlessness radiated in his cell.

Speaking in faith (faith-talking) makes your courage level rise. When we speak *and* model faith to one another, courage seems to grow exponentially.

If you are facing a storm—and who isn't?—do your best to surround yourself with fearless people.

A ROVING REVIVAL

These faith lessons were burned into me as we began to hold revival services as part of our Cover the City in Glory tour. Our first stop was a church in Gardner, near the southwest corner of Kansas City. When we arrived on the first night, people were lined up halfway around the building to get in. They had traveled from all around the city and fourteen different states to be there.

It took a couple of songs to get the sound system set correctly, but after that the Spirit began to flow freely. It was just like being at home—except that people who would never have been able to journey to Smithton had come to these meetings. Before the weekend was over, many were healed, saved and delivered. But I wondered, *Would there be lasting fruit? Or would our visit come and go like so many other church events?*

The answer came the next weekend when we set up at a Vineyard church in the northern part of the city. There in the crowd was a large group from Gardner, and they were helping to park the cars and usher and pray for people at the end of service. Now it was their turn to experience the other side of revival!

The pastor of the Gardner congregation opened the meeting with a testimony. He said that people in his church had never been this excited about Jesus before. Before the revival, he could hardly get anyone to do anything. Now they were ready to help in any way.

To me it was a sign that God had ministry for us on the other side of the storm. If we had been too afraid of venturing out, we would have missed these beautiful opportunities to touch lives.

Each week at each location we saw similar, wonderful results. All over the city, groups were gathering for prayer and to cry out for revival in the land. There were many manifestations of God's power. But the greatest thrill came when we saw men and women standing at the same altar where they had stood for years—but now they were filled with the fire of God. Not just that, but it was happening at their own church, not at a convention center.

We carried the fruit from church to church and pastor to pastor. Each church found its congregation growing in numbers, in love, in finances and in commitment to Jesus.

Our time of wandering continued, but we learned what it meant not to fear the storm and to stay the course as God guided us through.

CALLED ACCORDING TO HIS PURPOSE

One of the things that made the wandering time bearable was my awareness that God had a purpose for the church and for me on the other side. I'm sure you've been in those desperate places where you get so low you wonder if God is finished with you. I have been there. I remember those chilling days when I thought the move of God was coming, but that I would be left out because I was broken and unfixable.

If God starts you on the adventure, He'll lead you through! Not only that, but He'll also multiply and magnify your purpose as you show yourself faithful and committed.

One marvelous thing about the present-day revival is that Christians are being reintroduced to their life purpose.

People who thought God had given up on them, or who were hiding out in the back pew, are emerging as gifted and powerful leaders.

Of course, this should not surprise us. Romans 8:28 says:

And we know that in all things God works for the good of those who love him, who have been called according to his purpose.

That is one of my favorite scriptures in the Bible because it's a reminder that God is always up to something. He is always trying to produce good in your life and in mine. Even during the times when we have to learn a hard lesson, or when things don't happen as quickly as we want them to happen, God is doing good for us.

God didn't call us to a purpose because we earned that purpose. When God calls us, He does it according to *His* purpose. He does not call us according to *our* purpose, talent, ability or past performance. He calls us because He has something to accomplish.

Throughout history God has chosen leaders according to His purpose. He first creates His plan. Then He chooses the person He wants to carry out His plan.

There was one moment when He wanted to flood the earth and save the righteous. He needed someone—a preacher of righteousness—to build an ark, gather the animals and save a remnant of humanity so He could start over.

Suddenly Noah found his calling in God's purpose. He wasn't called because he was a great shipbuilder or zookeeper. *He was available.* God had a plan; Noah became His man.

Joseph's brothers threw him into a well. But God turned it into good because He had a purpose to save Egypt from famine and to rescue the family that would yield the Messiah.

Several generations later, God heard the cry of His people in slavery. He needed a leader to lead them out of Egypt to the Promised Land. He had a purpose, so he called Moses. Moses was not called according to speech or preaching abilities, but because God had a purpose.

Every great man or woman of the Bible was called according to God's purpose. *You and I are the same.* Sometimes we go to church believing that God's reason for being is to holler at us about watching too much television. But His purposes are much greater than that. He is calling us according to His purpose. He has a plan for you!

YOUR PURPOSE

God is up to something today—thousands of things. *Millions* of things. He is restoring honor to His name so that people will tremble at it rather than laugh at it on the silver screen.

He is calling people to follow the fire.

He is preparing a bride suitable for His Son, one who complements His glory.

He is building a church that will fight for His interests.

God has more of a purpose for you and me than simply working, eating, playing and throwing in a dash of church every week! When people were called in Bible times, they turned into brave, valiant, powerful leaders and went on great adventures. They became warriors, lion-fighters, spies, prophets, heads of state and generals.

When we are called according to His purpose, our lives should never be the same again.

When we have grasped the purposes of God for our individual lives—and for our churches—we will no longer go on as if God is a no-show landlord of the earth. We will no longer make plans or goals out of the thoughts in our head or build churches while giving only passing thoughts to what God wants.

We will no longer put up with the blandness of day-to-day living that is unconnected to anything meaningful.

Today is the day of God's purpose in your life. This is the hour of visitation, when unknown gifts and talents should be springing up in you. He has a purpose for you—and for me. How do we get hold of it?

NOT MANNA ANYMORE

One of the problems plaguing revivals of today is the manna mentality. This is the idea that revival will fall from heaven and we only need to be passive receivers of miracles. The truth is, God has ushered in a new era. We aren't in the days of manna anymore. He has put revival in our hands, but the miracle depends on us.

In Luke the story is told of the feeding of the five thousand. It is one of the best-known miracles of the New Testament and is told in all four Gospels:

When the apostles returned, they
reported to Jesus what they had done.
Then he took them with him and they withdrew
by themselves to a town called Bethsaida, but the
crowds learned about it and followed him. He
welcomed them and spoke to them about
the kingdom of God, and healed those
who needed healing.

Late in the afternoon the Twelve came to him
and said, "Send the crowd away so they can go
to the surrounding villages and countryside and
find food and lodging, because we are in a
remote place here."

He replied, "You give them something to eat."

*They answered, "We have only five loaves
of bread and two fish—unless we go and buy
food for all this crowd." (About five
thousand men were there.)*

*But he said to his disciples, "Have them sit
down in groups of about fifty each." The
disciples did so, and everybody sat down. Taking
the five loaves and the two fish and looking up
to heaven, he gave thanks and broke them. Then
he gave them to the disciples to set before the
people. They all ate and were satisfied, and the
disciples picked up twelve basketfuls of
broken pieces that were left over.*
—LUKE 9:10–17

The scene is familiar to anyone who has gone to church
or Sunday school. There were great crowds that day, and
they were in a remote place with nothing to eat. They had
been listening to Jesus so intently that their appetites took
a backseat to their interest in the gospel.

This was not the first time God faced a problem involving big crowds in the middle of the wilderness who were
wandering, hungry and in need of daily sustenance.
Hundreds of years earlier the children of Israel were stuck
in a desert and would have died without food. God's solution then was to feed them with manna from heaven, which
came down like dew and formed into cakes on the ground.

Now Jesus, the Son of God, faced a similar problem,
though there were not as many people as with the children of Israel. The most logical thing, in light of the
manna miracle of the Old Testament, would have been for
God to send manna from heaven again. He had done it
before. Why not now?

But Jesus did not call down manna from heaven. I believe that tells us something significant: The days of manna are past. Jesus could have called for manna, but it was not right to do it. It would not have fit what God was doing. It would have sent a wrong message.

Instead, Jesus said to the disciples, *"You* give them something to eat."* With His instruction, Jesus was signaling to the disciples that something new was going on. A change in the way God would work with His followers was taking place before their eyes.

Of course, in the natural the disciples began to think, *Where are we going to get enough food? If we have to feed all these people out of our own pockets, it's going to cost us.* But Jesus had other plans—plans to move out of the natural into the supernatural. The Book of John says there was a boy there that day who had five loaves and two fish. These loaves were not the long French loaves we see sticking out of baskets in some picture books. They were little, flat loaves. And the fish were not canned or prepared, but were probably hanging on a string as he carried them around all day.

I can imagine Jesus sitting back with amusement and watching the disciples try to solve the problem. He put the impossible situation in their hands because He was teaching them how things were going to work in the kingdom from that point on. Instead of God sending manna from heaven, He was going to put the power in the hands of regular people.

USING WHAT YOU HAVE

The first lesson this teaches us is to use what we have, even though it may appear not to be enough. We live in an age when God does not want us to wait for the manna from heaven. He wants us to use normal, everyday provisions to do the work of the kingdom. That means that revival doesn't need to wait until you find a star evangelist or the perfect worship leader or a gap in everybody's schedule. It can start right now with what you have.

If we in Smithton had waited for the right materials, we would still be waiting. Revival would have blown over like a three-day praise rally. We would have lost our moment of visitation.

Our church building was one of the oldest buildings in the county—a structure held together with wooden pegs, not nails. Our new gym, intended for volleyball games, became our makeshift sanctuary when visitors came. In winter it got so hot with so many people packed into the gym that we had to run the air conditioning. In the summer it was sweltering, and we countered the heat with more air conditioning and some store-bought fans.

We didn't have the best sound system or instruments or chairs. We had limited parking and no means of accommodating the traffic that came. People were forced to park along the streets.

And that does not include the spiritual hurdles. We had no revival manual telling us how to behave as ushers, altar workers, worship leaders and prayer teams. I didn't know how to preach five and six times a week.

Everything about our church—our facilities and talents—was humble. But God used it. Somehow we got it into our heads that we would use what we had until God gave us more, and that has been the pattern for us ever since.

Are you waiting for the right time to have revival? For school to get out? For additional vacation time from work? For a bump in pay?

Are you waiting for your church to finish its new sanctuary? Or lay new carpets? Or hire a better worship leader? The lesson from that mountainside is to see ministry in the impossible.

Another lesson we learn from Jesus in this story is that

God wants us to use *whom* we have. Jesus had only twelve waiters to serve five thousand men plus the uncounted women and children. But He went forward with total confidence and got the job done.

In our church we didn't have the money to bring in superstar staff people from outside. Why would people want to leave their own places to join us in the middle of rural Missouri? All of our staff, except for Kathy and me, were volunteers when revival began. Our worship leader drove a forklift for more than a year after revival started just to make a living, even as the songs he penned went around the world.

For years our congregation functioned in revival with fewer than three hundred people. Yet we prayed for, preached to and led worship for hundreds of thousands of visitors.

Churches shouldn't wait until they become "mega" to serve the masses. God has a purpose *now*, not next week. We must get the job done with what—and whom—we have, not what we think we need.

İN THEİR HANDS

The story continues, and we know it well. The disciples gave that little boy's fish and bread to Jesus. He looked up to heaven, gave thanks, broke the bread—and nothing happened. The food was very blessed; it had been offered to God with thanksgiving, but there were still thousands of hungry people and only a few morsels of food.

Remember, He didn't say, *"I'll* give them something to eat." He said, *"You* give them something to eat." All four Gospels say it that way. Jesus broke it and gave thanks, but the miracle didn't happen in His hands. *It happened in the hands of the disciples.*

What does that tell us about revival? It tells us that we had better not stand around waiting for manna to fall, because the bread from heaven is already here. Jesus said, "I am the bread" (John 6:35). It is our job to get the bread to the masses.

Over the years I have heard many people say, "Revival is a sovereign move of God." I agree with that. I have seen Him move sovereignly in my own church for five years. But I also believe that when God moves sovereignly in the earth, as He is doing today, people have a choice to participate. If they don't, then the visitation will end for them. That's why it appears that God is moving in some places but not others. Some congregations are grabbing the opportunity while others are letting it slip away.

God's purpose is *now*. If we don't grab it now, it moves on. He is calling people to join immediately, not next week. Remember how two of Jesus' would-be disciples responded to the call?

> *He said to another man, "Follow me."*
> *But the man replied, "Lord, first let me go and*
> *bury my father" . . . Still another said, "I will follow*
> *you, Lord; but first let me go back and say*
> *good-by to my family."*
> —LUKE 9:59, 61

These men tried to delay the call of God upon their lives. They even had noble reasons, but God's purpose kept right on going. Rather than rise to the level of a Peter or John, they went on their way and lost the chance to make history. They will forever be nameless to us, but their example should be a strong warning.

God is not partial to certain churches or people. He does not like my church more than your church or me more than anyone else. The fact that He brought revival to my congregation is proof enough that He will choose anybody. Your church is probably in a bigger city, larger in size, with newer facilities than mine was. So what are you waiting for? In this day of visitation, He offers revival to anyone who will take it. Any church, any individual, any city. The difference between the "haves" and the "have-nots" is this—the "haves" are actively participating and letting revival come into their hands.

Knowing that we have a purpose in God gives tremendous confidence. Instead of standing with our arms in the air, gawking up at heaven, hoping something happens, we are assured that something will happen. We are not tense when we come to church, praying that God will visit us again. We don't ask ourselves if the Holy Spirit is going to move at a service, and we don't ask when the revival will end. That's like asking when your marriage will end. It will only end if one or both of you want it to end. And it's for sure that God doesn't want it to end!

A purpose is durable, ironclad, indestructible. The only way you can lose it is by not putting it to use. That is why revival is called an *outpouring,* not a *downpouring.* God is not raining down manna from heaven. God is sending out His power through regular people.

God wants to do miracles in your hands. Jesus is calling you to be a doer of the Word. The power will come from God, but it will take place in your hands.

AN EVERYDAY REVIVAL

Through the years hundreds of pastors have asked me to pray for them, and I do, and some go back and expect revival to fall out of the sky on their congregations. It doesn't work that way. They are looking for the manna and overlooking the fish and bread. They want *pow! Bam! Zoom!* They don't want to have to use what is already in their hands.

When revival began, I thought God would bring gifted pastors and leaders to help us pray and minister in the services. Yet to my surprise, unassuming single moms, factory workers and schoolteachers began to be used by God. While I was waiting for the "real" ministers to arrive, God was anointing the "smelly fishermen," the down-and-outers and those going nowhere within our congregation. Early in revival I learned God wants to use what we already have.

Eric Nuzum, a forklift driver in an area factory, had spent several years quietly sitting in our congregation. Three weeks before the revival began, we asked him to stand on the platform with our praise team and strum along lightly on his guitar. The night revival struck, he was leading praise and worship for the second time in his life. It was obvious to all of us that the Lord wanted Eric to take up the challenge of learning to lead. As he yielded his abilities to the Lord, he was empowered, and giftings that he never dreamed of began to surface. God enabled him to set an anointed atmosphere where the presence of the Lord moved. And then he began writing wonderful original music on his forklift at work. Soon, God elevated this "smelly fisherman forklift driver" to the full-time staff position as music minister. Now, more than five years later, Eric is a well-known worship leader, and his music has been distributed by Integrity's Hosanna! Music all around the world.

Our job—your job and mine—is to use what we have, use whom we have, open our hands, our hearts, our eyes and let them be filled with what God has to give us. We must let many things go, but then we will begin to see miracles happening *through* us, not just *to* us.

Revival is the sovereign move of God working through earthly vessels. We have work to do. Don't be afraid of having the miracle in your hands or in your church or in your pastor's hands. If you continue to be a spectator, if you continue to be an audience, if you continue to try to be a third party because you don't want to ruin your reputation and you don't want somebody to criticize you, then you're missing the point.

Revival is a God-ordained move placed in the hands of man. When I figured that out, it changed my life and my ministry forever. I realized that my responsibility was not to drum up the power of God—that can't be done—but to work with all my heart, mind and soul with what He had already given me. Then the miracles started happening.

All kinds of healing began. Our entire congregation was learning to establish the presence of the Lord through intense praise and worship. With His presence comes His power to touch hearts and bodies.

The most major miracles were those of the soul. What I had tried to do by years of teaching, preaching and counseling the same people, the Lord was now accomplishing in a matter of moments with lightning bolts of His power. Bad attitudes, habits and sin patterns were being broken.

As the power of God swept through one night, a young man who was suicidal and hooked on drugs was powerfully touched. He testified the next week of a totally sound mind, with complete freedom from his addiction.

One weekend a fractured family came to the revival services, giving God one more chance before the husband followed through on a divorce. The presence of the Lord melted the husband's heart, freeing him from years of anger and bitterness. Restored, that family has been thrust into powerful ministry.

I have said it before: There is no shortage of new wine today. But there is a shortage of wineskins. There is a shortage of people who will be the vessels of God. No shortage of water—just a shortage of water jars.

After the miracle of the loaves and fishes, Jesus put His disciples into the boat and left them to go up the mountainside to pray. The Bible says, "They had not understood about the loaves; their hearts were hardened" (Mark

6:52). The disciples didn't have a *hand* problem—they had a *heart* problem. Their hands were fully functional for God's miracle-working power, but their hearts were blind.

People today can be the same way. When revival doesn't happen, often there's nothing wrong with the hands of the people who miss it, but there is something wrong with their hearts.

If we are to achieve the purpose to which God has called us, we must get our hearts right and open our hands to His power. Revival won't happen *to* you until you're willing to let it happen *through* you.

WHAT HAS SEİZED YOU?

Luke records the inspiring account of the transfiguration of Jesus on the mountaintop. By anyone's standard, those moments must be considered a visitation of the greatest order. God's presence was so strong that Jesus' clothes literally shone like lightning.

Then Jesus, along with Peter, James and John, who had been witnesses to the transfiguration, came down from the mountain and were met with a new challenge. A crowd had gathered, and a man whose son was demonized was asking the other disciples to deliver his son. But the disciples were unable to do so. (See Luke 9:28–45.)

What a contrast between what had just happened on top of that mountain and what was happening at the bottom! On the top of the mountain, Jesus was dazzling white in God's glory and speaking to Moses and Elijah. He was seized by the presence of God.

At the bottom was a boy, representing the world, who was seized by evil spirits.

At that time, the people of Israel were like that demonized boy—seized by the destroyer. They were sick, oppressed, full of demons. They were about as far from the purposes of God as you can be.

Some church people today find themselves and their families far from His purposes, too. They are seized by drugs, divorce, greed, halfheartedness toward God. They are supposed to be free, but the same curses that are afflicting the world have afflicted many Christians.

The world is pleading with God with the same words the father of the demonized boy used to plead with Jesus: "We begged Your disciples to drive it out, but they could not. We are seized and need help! Our children are shooting each other. Our morality is down the tubes. Our secular ideas of right and wrong haven't worked. Now we are seized by the destroyer—and nobody can help us."

The Holy Spirit is blowing across the land, melting people's hearts, causing them to hunger for spiritual things. But if we have been seized by the destroyer, we will have no spiritual solutions to give to people when they bring their problems to us—all we will have is a pat on the back and a counseling group.

Revival is about getting seized by the power and presence of God, then setting people free who are seized by the destroyer. That's what Jesus did that day. But the story did not end there.

Jesus delivered the boy from the demon, but He also expressed frustration:

O faithless and perverse generation,
how long shall I be with you and bear with you?
Bring your son here.
—Luke 9:41, NKJV

He was frustrated because He knew something that no one else knew: He knew He would be going back up the mountain—this time to a cross of crucifixion. Then He would be glorified again, as He had been in the transfiguration, but this time it would be forever.

He would no longer be there in person to help the demon-possessed, the hungry, the oppressed. He would not walk the dusty roads of Galilee or preach to the throngs in Jerusalem. He would not be available when the crowds went looking for Him in the evening.

How could He continue to help them? The only long-term solution was to put that power in the hands of His followers, beginning with the disciples. That is the purpose to which we are called. We are called to learn from Him and to free people who are seized by the destroyer.

Don't allow your hands to be so crowded with your own purposes that you have no room for God's purposes. Fill your hands and your life with the purposes of God. Let your hands be full of miracles, overflowing with healing, intercession, deliverance, wisdom and comfort.

Each of us can answer the call. You and I can be called to a life of biblical proportions if we are willing to be called to His purpose.

TEN

THE MINISTRY OF THE VOICE

Every week someone asks me a question along these lines:

"What do you think my ministry is?"

"How can I grab hold of God's purpose in my life?"

"I want to serve God, but what do I do first?"

There is nothing more exciting to see than an open and ready heart, and so I am glad to help these people find their answers. I usually do not know what ministry someone has been given from God just by talking to that person, and I am keenly aware that God hasn't appointed me to tell everybody who asks me what their purpose is. But even without knowing a person, I can always recommend one ministry all of us should accept—the ministry of the voice.

Voice ministry is a sign of the Last Days. In Acts 2:21, Peter quoted the prophet Joel, who said:

> And everyone who calls on the name of
> the Lord will be saved.

This announcement heralded the beginning of the Last Days. The main hallmark of the Last Days is that people will use their voices to declare and expand the kingdom—speaking, prophesying, singing, shouting, declaring, speaking in tongues, interpreting, encouraging, praising, worshiping and crying out. All of these expressions involve the use of vocal cords.

The sign on the Day of Pentecost that gave evidence that the one hundred twenty people in the upper room had been filled with the Holy Spirit was that each person began speaking in other tongues, "declaring the wonders of God." The early church was full of the ministry of the voice, with "songs, hymns and spiritual songs," prophecies, tongues and interpretations of tongues.

Do you see how the voice has become a tool for salvation and the spreading of the gospel? Yes, it was important before New Testament times to speak about the things of God and to remind each other of His ways, but it has become critical now. If we don't use our voices, we won't fulfill God's purpose.

WE NEED VOİCES!

Voice ministry is the first ministry a believer should have, and yet it is one of the most underdeveloped. People feel free to chat about the weather or sports or the stock market, but when it comes to using that same voice to minister to the Lord, they grow strangely quiet.

God has always had men and women who would speak for Him, going all the way back to Noah who was called a preacher of righteousness. Without the ministry of the voice we wouldn't have the Bible, because much of the Old and New Testaments were spoken before they were written down. Jesus' entire ministry consisted of speaking.

One aspect of the ministry of the voice is declaring who God is and removing obstacles to His presence. John the Baptist said that he was "the voice of one calling in the desert, 'Prepare the way for the Lord'" (Matt. 3:3). He was quoting the prophet Isaiah, and his words were intended to bring righteousness to Israel before Jesus began His ministry.

This use of the voice is a picture of honor. In ancient times, when royalty would go on a journey, servants would go before them to level out the path, removing stones and rocks. The low places would be raised up and the high places brought down. It was the servant's job to remove all obstacles so that the king or queen could make a smooth and easy entrance.

That is what John the Baptist did, and it is what we should do in our church services and in our private lives. We should constantly be removing every obstacle for our King. When we call for His entrance into our lives, we want our hearts to be free of stony places. We will not make Him find us in the valley of despair or on the mountain peak of pride, but we will build a level path with praise, worship, prayer, songs, hymns and spiritual songs.

LEARNING TO SPEAK

The first step in developing the ministry of the voice is to discipline the voice. If I handed a microphone to a person whom I selected randomly during a church service somewhere in America, and asked that person to say something on behalf of the kingdom, chances are he would be completely caught off guard and confess, "I don't have anything to say."

But up to that moment, he would have been saying a lot—analyzing in his heart, giving opinions, judging. But hand that person a microphone and say, "Let's hear what God has to say," and too many times the flow of words would stop. Why? Because no one can speak for God when he or she has been continually speaking for himself or herself all day long.

Many people have been unable to receive the gift of the Last Days because they haven't separated themselves from their own voices. They fill their hearts with the things of earth, so when an opportunity comes to speak for God, the wrong kinds of words come bubbling up.

It is a tragic fact that Americans are great opinion makers—but often we are not speaking for God nearly as much as we are speaking for ourselves. We're not expressing the desires of God. The world is ready to hear a message from the throne, but some Christians grow fainthearted, and their voices fall silent.

People fail as speakers for God when they don't discipline their self-talk. Don't speak out of your own thoughts—they may be filled with human qualities of bitterness, anger or fear. Those who are able to speak the voice of God are people who practice what His voice is saying to them day by day in their private lives, marriages and homes as parents, leaders and friends. You do it by listening to God and expressing the thoughts of God. Even if you never get asked to speak in front of a crowd, you can still be a sign of the Last Days as long as you speak God's mind all the time, even to yourself.

CALLING ON
THE NAME OF THE LORD

Growing in the ministry of the voice requires actually using our voices. Acts 2:21 says, "And everyone who *calls* on the name of the Lord will be saved" (emphasis added). We have to *call* on the name of the Lord. We can't simply think real hard about it or just express an earnestness in our heart. We have to speak it. We have to open our mouth, send air through our vocal cords and speak.

Often the first thing visitors notice about our church is the noise level. If you walked in one minute after worship had started, you would be surrounded by yelling, cheering, praising people whose voices could almost lift the roof off the building. Do they do it for effect? No; they do it because they have come to realize that the ministry of the voice is one of the most important aspects of revival.

It's easy to spot the visitors in such a crowd. They look around sheepishly, or even stay seated, and have embarrassed smiles. It's almost as if their discretion is being violated, or they think church should be a quiet place. After a while they have a change of heart. Soon they are standing up and clapping, and they may even raise their hands. If they stay for a couple more services, they begin to blend right in, and you hear their voices right along with everyone else's.

Shouting to God and calling loudly on Him is liberating, and our church is one among many where you can join in without shame. When you do, you can feel the salvation of God come in a fresh way. It's like a release valve inside that opens up, allowing you to give and receive much more. It's the difference between sending praise up through a drinking straw and sending it up through a pipeline.

I had to learn the ministry of the voice like anyone else. In the religious tradition in which I was raised, any sort of bodily demonstration was considered demonic. If something happened in your mind, that was perfectly acceptable. If a special revelation or warmth came to your intellect or heart, that was allowed under my church's unspoken doctrine. But if you actually felt waves of joy in your body, or were inspired to cry out, lift hands or do anything involving the body or voice, the Christians I knew said it was probably the devil.

Years of wrong training like that have pulled our voices out of us. The men in the Gospels may have been made mute by demons, but Christians have been muted by false doctrine. Whole generations have come and gone with hardly a whisper, and the ministry of the voice has been put on the shelf to gather dust.

It affects nearly all of us. All you have to do is say, "Let us pray," and every Christian in the room will bow his head, close his eyes and even fold his hands. The idea is to shut the body down, close out the world and let our spiritual expression be merely a thing of the mind and heart.

The Bible gives us a totally different picture. It balances internal things, like thoughts and feelings, with external things, like the lifting of hands and shouting of praise to God. The psalms say to "clap your hands...shout to God with the voice of triumph!" (Ps. 47:1, NKJV). The Gospels tell us that Jesus lifted His eyes toward heaven, and He shouted His words to the crowd.

When people got around Jesus, they shouted, too. A leper who was healed "came back, praising God in a loud voice" (Luke 17:15). When Jesus entered Jerusalem on the Sunday before Easter, the Bible says:

The whole crowd of disciples began joyfully to praise God in loud voices for all the miracles they had seen: "Blessed is the king who comes in the name of the Lord!" "Peace in heaven and glory in the highest!"

Some of the Pharisees in the crowd said to Jesus, "Teacher, rebuke your disciples!"

"I tell you," he replied, *"if they keep quiet, the stones will cry out."*
—Luke 19:37–40

Jesus wasn't interested in making everyone talk in a whisper—or with showing no bodily expression of what He felt. He wanted people to lay hold of the kingdom *with their voices.* Many of the people He healed were those who had kept on shouting until they got His attention. He rewarded their perseverance. The fear we have of using our voices—or our bodies—needs to be overcome if we are to fully participate in this visitation of God.

This truth came alive to me as I read scriptures that say, "Offer your *bodies* as living sacrifices" (Rom. 12:1, emphasis added). As a young Christian, I had to learn to trust my spirit, body and voice to God. I came to the point in my life of saying, "I'm so desperate. I have to trust You with everything—even my body and my voice."

It's not that God likes to hears us jabber or shoot the breeze. But He does fill our mouths with words worth speaking. As Last-Days Christians, we have words that we did not have before, expressing things that were not expressed before. We are the ones who call out the mighty things of God.

You may have been around "hush-hush religion" so much that you've lost your desire or ability to call. Maybe you never had it. But I guarantee that within you is the desire to call on God's name. He gives the desire and the ministry to every person who receives Him.

Try it out! Give a shout. Go into a room and shut the door so you can practice, then speak something out boldly, like, "God has not given us a spirit of fear, but of power and love and a sound mind!" Pick another verse that suits you and do the same thing, listening to your voice and gaining confidence in it. You don't have to like the sound of your own voice. Who does? But you have to learn to enjoy the feeling of speaking the words of God.

If you are a quiet worshiper at church, try breaking the mold a little bit. Stand next to someone loud, and try lifting your own voice. I can almost assure you that your spirit will leap inside of you like a horse set free from its stable.

AN OPEN HEAVEN

Prayer is another major aspect to the ministry of the voice. Effective prayer is like having an open heaven over your head. Ineffective prayer is like having heavens of brass. What we speak when we pray makes the difference.

As God's soldiers, we must have an open heaven above our heads. What could be worse for the field soldier than to be cut off from his commanding officer and unable to receive fresh orders? Yet, most of us have experienced "prayer that goes nowhere." It is as though our prayers are nothing more than an underarm lob that falls well short of heaven. Unfortunately, many of us spend our entire prayer lives speaking words into the air with little effect.

This described my life for many years. I wanted prayers that opened heaven, so I tried all sorts of approaches. I claimed promises. I bound and loosed things. I prayed scriptures. I waited silently on the Lord. But every time I threw my requests up, they came crashing back to earth. I had a few good moments over the years, but nothing approaching consistency.

Then I began to think about Matthew 6:8 where Jesus says, "Your Father knows what you need before you ask him." I asked God very sincerely, "If You already know my need, then why am I spending so much time talking about it?"

Over the course of a few months it began to dawn on me: Maybe prayer is not about my need. Maybe it's about something else, and I have been speaking the wrong things.

I read further in Matthew 6 and saw how Jesus taught us to pray: "Our Father in heaven, hallowed be your name." Now I was on to something! Prayer was about putting honor in to the airways. I was right back to the purpose and reason that we are here on the earth in the first place—to establish the honor of God, which was disrupted by Satan's rebellion.

The more I studied prayer, the more I became convinced that true prayer is not about my need. It is about God's honor. My need should only be a part of the conversation I have with Him. I began to approach prayer times with a new goal—to send honor into the pathways of earth and into the airways of heaven. I called forth the establishment of His kingdom and His will on this earth in my prayers, just as it is in heaven.

My prayers began to work! I no longer had the failed-rocket feeling. My words seemed to zoom right into the stratosphere and touch God's heart. No longer did I waste my words as the pagans do, who think God will hear them if they speak more. I focused my purpose on making His paths straight, declaring His glory. I made it my goal to get God's desires into my heart and then send them forth through the ministry of the voice.

Do I ever get around to talking about our needs? Of course I do. But by the time I establish an open heaven by declaring and interceding for the purpose of God, I can say in just a few seconds, "Give us today our daily bread." Prayer can include needs without being about needs. Instead, my voice becomes an instrument of glory that causes the heavens of brass to collapse and the doorway of heaven to open.

LEARNING TO GROAN

How should our prayers and declarations sound?

How do the prayers of a mother praying for a sick child sound? When a deer darts onto the highway in front of your car and you spontaneously call to God, what does that sound like?

The sound is real. The heart cry is real. No one has to analyze or evaluate it. Real prayer never has to be taught.

When God's heart gets inside your heart, the ministry of the voice is the result.

I learned to use my voice for God in an even deeper way during one particularly painful life experience. Before revival hit, our church had begun to have a new spark. Our prayer meetings had become the liveliest time of the week, and the people in the church were more committed than ever.

But a few relationships began to fall apart. Some people were not happy about the "new church," and they began to meet privately to discuss how to stand against the move of God. I tried to woo these people by giving them extra attention and inviting them to dinner. I would look for them after a service and try to strike up a conversation.

Then one couple called a private meeting, saying they wanted to iron out our differences. It turned out to be a blast of accusations that made little sense, but it tore the relationship further apart.

I spent a lot of time alone in prayer during those days, but even there I found little solace because God chose that time to deal with my own character. One night as I was facedown beside my bed trying to pray, a breeze of conviction swept over me. Words were forming in my mind that I wasn't sure I really wanted to hear. "There is something wrong with you," I heard the Holy Spirit say to my heart. "There is something wrong with your character. You get upset about the lies people are telling about you, but you are not the least bit bothered about things that are true, which no one knows about. You are faulted in your character."

I didn't enjoy hearing those words, but I accepted them. It was a correct evaluation. I answered back, "It's true; everything You have said is right."

Up until then I had not reached the "bottom of the barrel" in my spiritual experience. Suddenly, that was exactly where I found myself. My pious attempts at praying made no difference to God. Suddenly I knew it didn't matter if my hands were folded and my head bowed when I prayed. Somehow I knew that even if I spoke in perfect King James English, God would not be impressed. The only kind of prayer that would dig me out of the pit into which I had fallen was honest prayer.

That night I prayed deep groaning prayers that arose from deep inside my being. "Lord, save me," I cried out. "Rescue me. Have mercy on me, Lord."

My voice began to work in ways I had never known before as I reflected on the truth of what was in my spirit. There were no more cover-ups.

Those are the kind of heart-prayers that touch the heart of God. They are spirit-to-Spirit contact. Sometimes God gives us words, but sometimes we have only groanings. Those groanings bring relief to the soul and fill a deep need to have our deepest hurts understood and heard by God.

There are times for articulate praying and times for groaning; times for loud praying and times for soft praying. In any situation, prayer is foundational to the ministry of the voice.

The ministry of the voice is not optional. You don't speak for God just when you feel like it—you speak for God when He calls you to do so. You don't worship or pray when you feel like it. You do it regularly and often because that is what real life is about. It's not about you or me, your church or my church. *It's about Him.* The point of your voice ministry is to bring honor to His name.

When we do, we become voices in the wilderness for God—an entire "John the Baptist contingent" saying, "Make way for the Lord!"

ELEVEN

HOW TO ADVANCE İN THE SPİRİT

İf revival has touched your life, one of the greatest desires you may have today is a longing to advance in the things of God. Everywhere I go people want to know how to move ahead in the Spirit. They say things like:

- ❀ "I want to press into His presence."

- ❀ "I want to move to the next level."

- ❀ "I want everything God has for me."

All these sayings are different ways of reaching for the same thing. The first thing I encourage the people to do is what we discussed in the last chapter: Use your voice, fine-tune your self-talk, listen for the heart of God and then declare it whenever you can.

Then I tell them about three basic principles that help people to advance in the Spirit.

FİRST PRİNCİPLE: LOSE AS MUCH AS YOU CAN

It's hard to think of someone who advanced in the Spirit more completely than Paul. His words came to be considered the very words of God. How did he get so far? What was his secret? It was this: Instead of trying to gain everything, he tried to lose it.

If America had a corporate slogan, it would be, "Gaining is everything." Listen to the conversations at any coffee shop, and you hear people talking about capital gains, gains realized from a business transaction, gaining muscle tone, gaining influence. Nobody talks about the benefits of losing anything (except weight!).

Most people approach their spirituality with the same mind-set. They want to gain God while hanging on to as much as they can from the world. After all, more is always supposed to be better than less.

Think of a child who is offered a new toy when his hands are already full of toys. What does he do? He shoves the handful of toys into his pockets, then takes the new one!

When people receive Christ they often have the same response. They take the world's trinkets and souvenirs and stuff them in their pockets so they can have them for later. People who have tasted revival may do the same thing, receiving as many of the blessings as they can while still hanging on to the world.

The apostle Paul turned modern ideas of profit and loss upside down. In his economy, earthly loss meant heavenly gain. He was willing to lose all things—*all things*—so that he might gain the fullness of Christ.

*But whatever was to my profit I now
consider loss for the sake of Christ. What is
more, I consider everything a loss compared to
the surpassing greatness of knowing Christ Jesus
my Lord, for whose sake I have lost all things. I
consider them rubbish, that I may gain Christ and
be found in him, not having a righteousness of my
own that comes from the law, but that which is
through faith in Christ—the righteousness that
comes from God and is by faith.*
—Philippians 3:7–9

He followed Christ's example, which was to give up everything, even life, in order to store up treasures in heaven.

*Then he [Jesus] called the crowd to him
along with his disciples and said: "If anyone
would come after me, he must deny himself and
take up his cross and follow me. For whoever
wants to save his life will lose it, but whoever
loses his life for me and for the gospel will
save it. What good is it for a man to gain the
whole world, yet forfeit his soul?"*
—Mark 8:34–36

Many believers today fumble along in their walk and don't know why. Many waste years trying to bring the toys from their old lifestyle into the kingdom with them. Paul's example—and Jesus' example—is not to hang on to as much as we can, but to lose as much as we can. That is a true measure of greatness in the kingdom.

One of my ministry "secrets" is that I don't get God to flow in my life by increase. Everything I get comes by decrease as James 4:10 says: "Humble yourselves before the Lord, and he will lift you up." If you could hear me praying by the side of my bed, you would know that I don't say, "God, let the power flow through me tonight. I need to feel that anointing." Instead I spend my time decreasing in myself, letting my words and my concerns be about Him. I allow myself to get smaller as He gets bigger in the eyes of my heart. Prayer for me is often not being pumped up with good feelings, but bottoming out and seeing again that I am nothing and He is everything. Only then does He bring victory and power into my life.

We talked earlier about God calling us according to His purpose. There is a reason Jesus has snatched your life from the miry clay. He created you to do something specific. Most people vaguely believe that, but never discover the reason. Why? I believe you won't ever get a clear look at your purpose until you are willing to lose everything you have. Then your life purpose will emerge from the midst of uncertainty.

This means being willing to give up not just "bad" rubbish, but also "good" rubbish. To most of us, forgetting our past means trying to forget all the bad things we did to someone or the things they did to us. We are perfectly willing to throw out old hurts and pains like yesterday's trash, but this is not what Paul meant. He was not forgetting his bad past, but his successful past. It was his "faultless" religion that was standing in the way of really knowing Christ. Opposition to God's visitation always comes from "faultless, self-righteous religion."

What successes have you had that keep you from advancing in the Spirit? What points of pride do you rely on instead of relying on Christ? A college degree? A well-paying job? A good-looking spouse? Any of these can become stumbling blocks if our confidence is placed in them.

The problem with success is that it makes people coast. Americans dream of winning the lottery or a game show so they can take it easy for the rest of their lives. Most of us have to work hard instead. Some work only for the goal of retiring early and coasting the rest of the way.

Paul could have coasted for the rest of his life on the accomplishments he had piled up as a young man. He was a shining star in the Jewish academic world. After meeting Christ he could have remained a student of the Law and nurtured a secret relationship with the Lord while continuing to advance among Jewish scholars.

But that wasn't his way. He piled up his successes and threw them onto the trash heap to be burned. They were only trash to him, compared to the privilege of knowing Christ.

And he didn't stop there. He pushed, pressed and sprinted until the day he died. We have all seen a runner going toward the finish line of an Olympic race with his neck and head straining forward. That last effort can be the deciding factor in who wins the race.

Too many churches teach a coasting kind of commitment. In fact, many are actually committed to coasting—they hold it to be their birthright to put their own lives in neutral, kick back and enjoy the ride whenever they feel like it. Leisure in our country is almost a sacred rite!

Most people will not strain themselves for anything. Some strain for lots of money, a high position in a company or early retirement. But who strains to win God's prize? Such a person is considered odd or fanatical.

Who will strain ahead for the prize of this high calling? Who will put the strain of sacrifice into the race?

Lose what you must lose. Forget what you must forget. Don't coast. Strain toward the prize until you take hold of that for which Christ Jesus took hold of you.

SECOND PRINCIPLE:
LISTEN TO THE "YES" IN YOU

I mentioned earlier that many people can't say yes to what God has for them because they haven't learned to say no to their other plans. Jesus put it this way in Matthew 26:40:

Then he returned to his disciples and found them sleeping. "Could you men not keep watch with me for one hour?" he asked Peter. "Watch and pray so that you will not fall into temptation. The spirit is willing, but the body [or the flesh] is weak."

God wants to do so much in the world, in your church and in your life. You can probably feel in your heart the activity of God. But when your body is too weak to keep up with your spirit, you have to cancel the plans God has for you. The activity of God is surging forth with amazing speed, but your body may be unwilling.

The good news is that the spirit is willing. There is a "yes" inside of you. Every single Christian has a "yes" inside of himself or herself. We all have willing spirits. In fact, your spirit, if born again, never rebels against what God wants to do. It is in absolute cooperation with God.

Not only that, but Jesus lives inside of you, and we know that He is willing. When Jesus met the man with leprosy, the leper said, "If you are willing . . . " Jesus said, "I am willing." The Holy Spirit resides in us and is willing, too.

Once we learn to say yes to our spirits and no to our bodies, we will have a lot going for us. My congregation and I learned this lesson when we started a corporate prayer meeting two and a half years before revival hit. Until that point we all thought we were pretty good pray-ers, but we learned that first night how out of shape we were. Our spirits were very willing to pray long and hard, but our bodies wanted nothing to do with it.

I remember telling the people, "We're going to pray for revival and for the presence of God to dwell here tonight." We all began to pray aloud, "Yes, Lord, send Your Spirit. We want Your Spirit . . . " Fifteen seconds later everyone had fallen silent! Where did our commitment to pray go? What happened to the prayer? The flesh put the brakes on it. It wasn't that we were unwilling— our spirits wanted to pray, but our bodies would only allow about fifteen seconds of it before shutting down.

So I started training all of us, myself included. I encouraged and prodded us to pray corporately for longer periods of time. I felt like a basketball coach standing on the sidelines, but in this game I was one of the players. We took Paul's exhortation seriously and began putting our bodies under subjection and training them to obey our spirit's command.

"We're going to tell our mouths to keep praising and not quit until the coach blows the whistle," I told our people. "Your mouths are going to want to quit, and your bodies are going to want to quit raising your hands. But tell your body, 'You don't tell me when to stop; I tell you when to stop.'"

After several months of this, we really were in shape. The "yes" inside of us was louder than ever before. Our bodies began to understand their proper places. We could pray for almost as long as we wanted to without dropping off.

Today people wonder how our church has such explosive praise and prayer. The secret is that we trained for it. When revival hit, we were ready to roll. That isn't always evident because the training happened a long time ago when nobody was watching us. Guests are unable to see the preparation that went into it. They say, "Oh, I see. The music starts, the power of God falls, and you start praying like that." No, we had been in training, and we were preparing for revival. We were preparing for the big game.

Remember that your spirit is always volunteering to do things for God—it's your flesh that says *stop*.

FUEL ECONOMY

Another aspect of listening to the "yes" inside of you is learning to conserve the energy God gives for the things that God wants. People sometimes ask me how I am able to schedule my life to keep from being busy all the time. I have learned to plan weeks and months ahead so that my calendar is full of things I know God wants me to do. Kathy and I call it *planning our fuel economy.*

I have decided I cannot afford to waste fuel on fleshly pursuits. I want everything I do to go in a *God*ward direction. Anything that wastes fuel is my enemy. For example, if I hear someone speaking negatively about others or tearing other people down, I shut my ears because processing that junk would take precious fuel. I need all the fuel I have for Jesus. I can't take excursions here and there, burning up fuel on things like petty anger, jealousy, worry or fear. Those things are from the flesh, and they get in the way of the "yes" in my spirit.

A man in my congregation flew a stealth bomber during his military career. He will tell you that as long as a pilot stays on mission, he will have enough fuel to return home. His commanding officer tells him, "Go there, blow that thing up and fly back." The pilot must perform the mission exactly according to the plans.

He can't fly along and say, "I don't like those people over there in that other place. Let's go blow them up first." If the pilot did that, he wouldn't have enough fuel to accomplish the real mission. He would run out of fuel and crash.

Many people can't figure out why they are crashing

spiritually. It's because they are taking excursions out of the Spirit of God and burning all their fuel. God is ready to send you on a mission. He has your day . . . your week . . . your life planned, but you may not have the fuel to accomplish the mission because you're bombing everything else, getting angry or planning all sorts of ungodly activity. You are saying "yes" to the flesh instead of to the spirit.

Don't take side missions! If your church has weekend meetings, budget your energy through the week so that you have plenty when Friday night rolls around. Say no to the frivolous things. Stay on course, and you will have enough fuel to accomplish everything God's mission requires.

THIRD PRINCIPLE: STAY UNIFIED

The hardest part about revival has nothing to do with learning how to handle the presence of God—the hardest part is keeping the spirit of division out of the church. I believe division is a spirit that is sent forth by the devil to whisper in people's ears and foment division where there should be none. There doesn't even have to be a real problem. It just takes someone with ears to hear what the spirit of division is saying.

One pastor I knew admitted hearing a voice telling him over and over again that I was building my own ministry on the back of revival. As he attended our revival services, he began to think, *Why should I be here building this guy's reputation? I have my own kingdom to worry about.* Soon he stopped coming to the services. His own ministry could have been richly blessed, but because he yielded to the voice of division, he drifted back to his own church, and we haven't heard from him since.

At our church, as in any church, there have been trying times when the devil sent wolves in among us. Wolves' activities are easy to recognize. They meet privately with others and try to insinuate that there is something wrong with the church's direction, theology or finances. Wolves don't offer loving criticism—they don't even have solutions to offer. But they love to put doubt in people's minds about the motives of the pastor and lay people who aspire to leadership.

Over the years I have discovered that it is nearly impossible to prove a motive. You almost always have to wait for a motive to manifest itself in an action. Then, if it's a wrong action, you can deal with it. But going hunting for wrong motives is like trying to catch water in your hand.

Yet some people can't help themselves. They want to pull up their lawn chairs and observe everything that happens in the church so they can ascribe wrong motives to certain people—especially to the pastor. They accuse pastors of having favorites in their congregations or of asking too much of people or of having a satanic theology. Often the criticism conflicts with itself and doesn't make internal sense. That has taught me a lesson about division: When division is from the devil, it hardly ever makes sense. It doesn't need to—it only needs to make people feel important, justified and proud.

I have seen people who once openly confessed their love for God lose their spiritual edge and their joy. I have seen them fall into a snare from which no amount of reasoning or preaching will free them. They go from being a wolf on the prowl to being a wolf caught in a trap, not letting anyone near to set them free.

Unfortunately, division happens everywhere. There doesn't have to be a revival or a fresh move of God for it to happen. Right now many people are attending churches that lack the presence of God but are full of division. They may not look divided. They may appear to be respectable, open, friendly and stable. But one day, people's true motives will be revealed, and out of nowhere the church will implode. Maybe it will be a fight over the finances, the color of the carpet or which evangelist to bring in. When a church is divided, it is like having a fault line that may not be visible but that can do a lot of damage in a small amount of time.

Some people say that revival brings division, but that is not really true. Revival only provides an opportunity for Satan to drive a wedge between people because of all the new things taking place. Revival doesn't cause division; it only reveals the division that has been hidden all along. When a visitation from God comes near, it shows how divided the church was already.

Jesus walked on earth with His chosen twelve disciples—one of whom was Judas, the disciple who eventually betrayed Christ. It was at the end of three years of ministry with Jesus that Judas revealed himself as a betrayer. I have learned that during times of God's visitation through revival today, "Judas" often reveals himself after three years.

As I have observed the move of God in revival upon our world today, I've seen revivals that went for two to three years in a honeymoon experience—all the people loved each other and felt the love of God powerfully in their corporate group. Everything ran smoothly—but then the honeymoon ended without any warning. The Judas spirit revealed itself from within. Sometimes it is not the fringe participants who exhibit this spirit; it is the people most trusted by the leadership. They have participated in revival, followed the fires of revival and testified of revival to others. What happened?

The truth is that nothing happened. Nothing has to happen. There is no event or argument that causes it. It happens because the whisperer has come and sown seeds of division. These people, once changed by the Spirit of God, are now changed back into suspicious, gossiping, faultfinding people.

It isn't the ones these people accuse who are harmed—it is they themselves who are harmed and destroyed by this spirit. They lose their joy. They lose their ability to connect with God. Though they once carried the Spirit of God to the nations, now they can no longer find God for themselves.

The end result is that division occurs. Despite the efforts of many, the Judas spirit causes these people to be divided against the very people who loved them.

In spite of the division caused by a Judas spirit, revival continues and grows in power. But I can't help thinking about all that people who develop a Judas spirit miss, and what our churches miss in their absence. What plan did God have for them? What would He have done with their ministry? Would the local church have reached more people if they had stayed? Only God knows.

Division wouldn't be so bad if people just drifted away from the church, but every leader knows that doesn't happen. Instead, people meet in dark corners, hold secret meetings and have private telephone conversations to air their feelings. It becomes evil at its highest level.

Like any church, we have had people who dropped out of the race along the way. Some wanted their old lives back. Others became offended by small, unimportant issues. There are many outward reasons why people change their minds, but most are just the kind of flimsy excuses that Jesus had to endure during His own earthly ministry. The bottom line is that not everyone wants to live on the edge of the flames, single-eyed and following a fire that they cannot control.

VIGILANT UNITY

Staying unified in revival is harder than staying unified without revival because the stakes are higher and the enemy puts more resources into messing with people. The ways to keep unity are not any different, though.

❀ *Speak healthy words.* Don't engage in conversations that undermine the church, the pastor or lay leaders. If you have a legitimate concern, take it to the pastor or to the relevant person. I have seen more division start in private conversations than any other way.

❀ *Test the spirits.* Sometimes the feelings or leadings you may have are not the Holy Spirit, but spirits of division. Test them. Is that grievance legitimate, or is it meant to be a wedge? Are you the only one who took offense at something? Do you have a solution in mind, or do you simply want to air your hurts? It is better to unmask divisive spirits before confronting someone about a perceived wrong.

❀ *Test yourself.* It is easy to see wrongs in other people, but harder to see them in ourselves. When you take an honest look at yourself first, it helps to give you clarity. Often you will find that your grievance wasn't that great after all, considering the work still being done in your own heart.

How do we advance in the Spirit?

❀ Lose as much of yourself as you can.

❀ Listen to the born-again "yes" inside of you.

❀ Stay unified.

If you keep these three principles, you will go far in the move of God and His purpose for you and your church.

PART III

TWELVE

GOD'S GLORY DESCENDING

▼

It's hard to describe what it feels like walking into a service charged with God's presence. Back in Smithton every inch of space in our building was being used. Those dear people, many of whom had lined up early in the day just to get in, would be packed shoulder to shoulder from the platform to the back door. Many had to be seated on the platform. Often I felt like rubbing my eyes and asking, "Am I really the pastor of this move of God?"

Today we have a bigger facility, but the power and glory of God still strike awe in me. Sometimes during a service we will see a hazy cloud or mist that is tangible. It may envelop the platform or a certain group of people. It seems to happen when there is a particularly powerful work of God taking place.

We can actually feel the weight of God's glory on our bodies. When we walk around during prayer time or worship time, it feels as if we're walking through an invisible but energy-filled substance. Sometimes our speech slows down, and it becomes hard to stand erect. Often we just want to lay on the ground and let the flood of God's glory wash over us.

When the glory of God comes down, it feels as though you can see clearer, deeper and further. You see more than people's actions—you see their hearts and motives. The unseen becomes more real than the seen.

Some nights I feel like a third person watching as God works so mightily. I know that I am the one leading the meeting or preaching, but I feel like just another face in the crowd. The power and presence of God has been manifested, and I have become a spectator watching it unfold right along with everyone else. How marvelous to be so involved and so removed at the same time. How wonderful to have something happening through me and around me, but not be *of* me.

Often I get a picture in my mind ahead of time of what God wants to do. Then it is only a matter of obeying and following what I have just seen in the spirit. It happens so fast, so powerfully and so easily. I might "see" pastors lined up at the front and the wind of God blowing like a breeze of refreshment upon them. Then all I do is call the pastors forward, and God does the rest. It happens just as I saw it happening a minute or two earlier.

Sometimes I see a wave of healing sweeping through the congregation. I simply tell the people that I sense healing in the house, and suddenly it happens.

As the pastor, I respond as a guide or an informant of the intentions of God. I have no power except to proclaim and watch it happen. It is like a dream come true. What happens in our midst is all about Him.

And more than anything, I want His glory to remain.

WHAT'S NEXT?

I am often asked what I think God will "do next" in revival. As people see seasons of manifestation come and go, they become hungry for more. Of course, no one but God knows what will happen next, but I have a hunch that it has something to do with His glory.

And we, who with unveiled faces
all reflect the Lord's glory, are being transformed
into his likeness with ever-increasing glory, which
comes from the Lord, who is the Spirit.
—2 Corinthians 3:18

I believe that at some point God is going to send so much glory that people will radiate and shine as Moses did when he came back from meeting with God. He would veil his face when the glory of God came upon him so that other people weren't frightened.

When Jesus was transfigured in front of Peter, James and John, even His clothes and face shone brighter than lightning.

His clothes became dazzling white, whiter
than anyone in the world could bleach them.
—Mark 9:3

The day is coming when we're going to see the glory of God descend from the throne of God onto churches. We're going to hear of manifestations of the glory of God shining on the faces and bodies of entire congregations around the world.

I don't wish for this because I want some new manifestation to marvel at. Some churches and movements today seem constantly to need something to run after. They've become bored with Jesus. "Do something to entertain us, God," their attitude says. They want new manifestations, new revival quirks, new oddities.

But after experiencing the glory of God, I don't want the latest thing. I want the eternal thing. He's more than enough. I don't need something "new" from heaven to entertain me. God's glory is all I want. And I believe it is coming in a much greater measure than we have already experienced.

Romans 12:2 says, "Be transformed by the renewing of your mind." The same Greek word being used in this verse for *transformed* is used by the Gospel writers when they write about Jesus being *transfigured* on the mountain. To me this signals that God wants more for us. To be transformed in the renewing of our minds, our habits and our goals is to reflect more of His glory. As we follow the fire more faithfully, we will see more of His glory.

WHEN THE GLORY COMES

The entire history of God's people shows us that God wants to descend on His people with glory. He wants to come down and dwell in your church, in your home, in your life and in your personal relationships.

In the first few verses of the Book of Genesis, the presence of God came down as the Holy Spirit hovered over the earth—even though the earth was still without form and had nothing in it. Does God want to send His glory to earth? Of course! He got here before we got here.

Since Creation a lot of things have happened to rob us of that glory. But we know that God is going to have the final say, because as we read the Book of Revelation, we find the glory of God returning to men:

*And I heard a loud voice from the
throne saying, "Now the dwelling of God
is with men, and he will live with them. They
will be his people, and God himself will be
with them and be their God."*
—REVELATION 21:3

Many sermons have been written about getting to heaven, yet so few sermons are about God's glory coming down today.

The children of Israel and the Jewish people in the days of Jesus' ministry on earth were not longing for salvation after they died—they wanted their salvation and their deliverance while they lived. Salvation was something that happened to people who were alive. It's the same with people today. The world is hurting so badly that they don't want to talk about "the sweet by-and-by"—they want to be rescued out of the nasty now-and-now!

And they can be! The answer is the visitation of God, which is releasing prisoners and breaking off all habits that have held us back. It is bringing the glory back to the church—and with that glory comes power to change, power to be transformed.

The Old Testament record shows us that God came down from season to season to manifest His glory among people. After mankind messed up God's plan to dwell with man, God initiated a plan to bring His glory back. He was working His plan from the time of Adam and Eve, but the reappearance of His glory started with one man— Moses—and a burning bush in the middle of the desert.

God wasn't satisfied with sending His glory to a bush in front of one man. He wanted a bigger visitation, so He came down on a mountain and appeared to the whole nation of Israel at once.

But God wasn't satisfied with that, either. He didn't

want to keep coming down to bushes or mountains, so He gave the Israelites a new plan. He told them to set up a tabernacle where He could come and dwell among men more permanently.

Before the tabernacle could even be begun, man was in trouble again. The Israelites grew impatient waiting for the glory, and they doubted God would come, so they made a golden calf. In response, God said, "Change of plans, Moses. I'm not coming down. I will send my angel instead."

Sometimes God seems to say things that contradict His real intentions. Moses knew God well enough to know that He wanted to send His glory down and that sending an angel was a second choice. Many of us might have backed away and said, "It's not God's timing. I guess we're not going to get the glory right now," but Moses made an appeal to God.

"If You don't come down, what is going to distinguish us from all the other people on the face of the earth?" he asked. In other words, Moses was saying, "An angel's OK, but it's not good enough. We have to have You. It's Your glory coming down that makes us different."

Wouldn't you like that to be the theme of your life—the theme of your church—today? Wouldn't it be nice if the leadership recognized the lack of glory and said to the congregation, "From now on there's a moratorium on everything we do"? How exciting if churches would assert, "Until God comes down we're not taking another step. This year the Easter Pageant, the children's play and the singing Christmas tree are all canceled unless God's glory comes down."

In effect, that's what Moses said: "Don't make us go on without Your glory." In response to Moses' plea, God relented and said He would come down in His glory. The people proceeded with their plans to build the tabernacle—following His specific instructions—and then the cloud covered the tent of meeting and the glory of the Lord indeed filled the tabernacle.

Through all the failures of mankind, that's exactly what God has always wanted to do. It's what He wants to do today in your church and every other church on the planet.

HIS PRESENCE OR OURS?

Thousands of churches are hungry for revival, but after four or five years of praying for it, many still haven't received it. Why? It's because their presence is taking up all the room.

Every person carries a presence. Some have a stronger presence than others, but everybody's presence sends signals to people around us and to God. Every married person knows this phenomenon: Our spouse has sonar, radar, a silent presence that sends invisible messages that we can hear, feel and read.

It's the same thing when we're talking about God. He has an invisible presence that we can learn to feel, hear and read, but we have to allow His presence to be the dominant presence in our life and church services.

People in a congregation sometimes try to dominate the church by their presence. Sometimes as a pastor preaches a strong message, a person on the board or someone who has been a part of that congregation for a long time begins to send out his or her signals. Suddenly, in the middle of his wonderful sermon the pastor finds himself in a spiritual battle. He begins to question, "Should I go through with this, or should I back down?"

One of the challenges of being a man or a woman of God is not to be dominated by the invisible presence of people, but to be moved by the presence of invisible God. Being dominated by people leads to becoming a people pleaser.

The desire of every man or woman of God, pastor and believer alike, is to be a carrier of the presence of God. For that to happen, your own presence is going to have to decrease. God is not going to place His presence on top of your presence. Rather, He will replace yours with His. You must want His presence more than you want your own presence.

For that to happen, you have to come into a service and "disappear." You will be there in body, mind and spirit, but as far as your own presence, your own opinions and your own feelings are concerned, they disappear.

Revival isn't about airing our own thoughts and feelings. God is not like a television talk show host who goes out in the audience with a microphone for feedback. He is exactly the opposite. We will be drinking in His ideas, His love and His presence forever and ever. That's what Christianity is about. Out of honor for Him, willingly, on purpose, we lay down our own presence to display His presence.

The most wonderful times I've ever had with the Lord have been times when I completely lost my presence and became absolutely abandoned to His presence. In all the annals of time, my presence—and your presence—will not prove important. We are each a mist, a vapor. Millions of people came before us, and if He tarries, millions will come after us. But His presence remains.

A PLACE FOR HIS GLORY

The Israelites built a tabernacle in obedience to God, but even that didn't satisfy Him. The day came when He said it was time to build a temple, a more permanent place for His glory and presence to rest. So Solomon built a temple, using massive amounts of metals, woods and precious stones. When it was finished, the same thing happened as did in Moses' day—God came down in His glory, which was so thick and powerful that the priests, accustomed to being in His presence, could not stand up.

Then the temple became the center of activity for the

Jewish people. For centuries it was the place for sacrifices and worship, but it was also the place for corporate prayer. The Jewish people joined often for prayer, and their prayer meetings were quite unlike some of the modest, quiet affairs you see at modern churches. People didn't kneel in the corner and bury their face in the pew so no one could hear them. Instead, they stood and prayed aloud. Hundreds of other people were praying like that at the same time.

The temple was the hub of all Jewish activity, full of God's glory and the prayers of His people. But once again, the people of Israel failed in their relationship with God and forfeited the presence of God. The people were led away captive. Many of them were taken away in chains. What Moses feared most came upon them—they lost their distinguishing mark of God's presence. The glory was gone. No one would recognize captured prisoners who were being taken away to bondage as the people of God! That is, no one but God! In the last book of the Old Testament, God promised to restore His glory to His people:

See, I will send my messenger, who will prepare the way before me. Then suddenly the Lord you are seeking will come to his temple.
—MALACHI 3:1

That is pretty good news to a people who have messed up, been captured and lost the glory of God. Throughout the long four hundred years of their captivity they lived with this promise ringing in their ears: "Someday the glory of God will return to the temple."

And it happened, although differently than they expected. This time the glory came in the form, not of a bush, a mountain, a tabernacle or a temple, but of a Man—Jesus. It was so different from what they expected that many of them didn't recognize it. God was putting His glory on a person—not on a place—and that Person was a model of the kind of glory God would send from that day on.

TOGETHER, WE ARE THE TEMPLE

Paul wrote in 1 Corinthians:

> *Don't you know that you yourselves
> are God's temple and that God's
> Spirit lives in you?*
> —1 Corinthians 3:16

The temple is the place where God visits and dwells. You are the temple. I am the temple. Together we are the temple, and if the Bible calls us the temple, then we should expect God's glory to descend.

When Paul says, "You are the temple," he is speaking in the plural, meaning that the local church is the temple. This manner of speaking characterized Jewish thinking. Rather than individualizing everything as Americans do, the Israelites applied the concept of temple to the corporate body, the community of believers. Paul wrote his words in 1 Corinthians to a whole church—not to one person.

In Ephesians 2:21–22 he reaffirmed this corporate thinking by writing:

> *In him the whole building is joined
> together and rises to become a holy temple in the
> Lord. And in him you too are being built together
> to become a dwelling in which God lives
> by his Spirit.*

In other words, we are temples for God at every level: individually, as a local church and as the church around the world.

Unfortunately, American teaching focuses almost entirely on the individual level, and we rarely learn how to be the temple as a local church. Think back to the different Sunday school classes you have attended. My guess is that nearly every one focused on a particular need or desire you had as an individual, but didn't really teach you how to behave and thrive as part of the church body. You were probably not taught to praise as a unit, pray as a unit or evangelize as a unit. But you probably heard a lot of teaching aimed at making you a happy single person, happy married person, happy young adult or happy senior citizen. Some churches spend a lot of time teaching people life skills based on their age or marital status, but not a lot of time teaching a church to behave as a church.

Paul's point is this: God created us to stand together as His temple—not to stand alone. Sure, we can have the glory of God in our individual lives. But in my experience, it cannot compare to a corporate anointing that can rest on an entire church. It is just as important—perhaps more important—that we be built as a local body into the temple of the Holy Ghost. I believe that is an important key to seeing His glory return.

The Bible says to be of one mind, or to start thinking as a body. God doesn't want to come down in His glory to visit us alone, but as a group. He has always dealt with people that way. Even Jesus, who was so personal and individual in His ministry, mostly taught the disciples as a group. After His resurrection He appeared to them when they were together, and He ascended before the twelve.

Yes, God sends His glory to us individually, but we will only see revival when we begin functioning as a local church with one heart and mind toward the things of God.

LİVİNG STONES

Can you imagine being able to see the glory of God coming down on groups of people all over the earth? Can you picture their faces glowing, as Moses' did, as they return to their neighborhoods and schools? What if you hardly needed to open your mouth to share the gospel because your face witnessed God's glory so much that the sight of it struck fear in the hearts of unrepentant men and women?

Today we get glimpses of God coming down in glory, but it is not happening on a large scale. I believe He wants it to! When wave after wave of God's glory is wafting down over all the world, the church will finally be distinguishable from all other people and religions.

Are you ready to be part of that temple? Are you ready to fit into a church body as one of many living stones? Are you ready to be part of a new kind of church with a new kind of thinking and new priorities? Paul wrote:

*By the grace God has given me, I laid
a foundation as an expert builder, and someone
else is building on it. But each one should be
careful how he builds.*
—I Corinthians 3:10

The foundation of each local church is Jesus Christ. Everything we do has to be built on Him. They did it in Paul's day, and we're doing it in our day, but everyone should be careful how he builds because we want to build the temple of God—not just awesome youth groups or dynamic outreaches. We are building a place where God will come and dwell.

*For no one can lay any foundation other
than the one already laid, which is Jesus Christ.*

*If any man builds on this foundation using gold,
silver, costly stones, wood, hay or straw, his
work will be shown for what it is, because the
Day will bring it to light. It will be revealed
with fire, and the fire will test the quality
of each man's work.*
—1 CORINTHIANS 3:11–13

We are the living stones, and Paul says we must build with the most costly materials we have. After all, we are taking about a temple for God, and only the best will do. Take the examples of Solomon and David in the temple they built for God. They gave lavishly from their personal treasuries to the building of the temple. Do we dare try to get by as cheaply as we can as we build the living temple of God in our day?

ROWING
AGAINST THE WIND

A lot of people find themselves rowing against the wind, as the disciples did in Mark 6.

*When evening came, the boat was in the middle
of the lake, and he [Jesus] was alone on land. He
saw the disciples straining at the oars, because
the wind was against them.*
—MARK 6:47–48

I'm sure that the disciples thought the devil was pushing them to the middle of the lake, trying to hinder their efforts to reach the opposite shore. That's like a lot of Christians who interpret every challenge as an attack from the enemy. However, it is really God who is putting us in a position to show His glory and nature. The strong wind is often the wind of His will, pushing us into the middle of the lake where we become witnesses of His glory. Our goal may be to get to the other side, but His goal is to show us a new dimension of who He is.

God prepares us for the return of His glory by showing us the futility of our efforts without it. It was Jesus who sent the disciples onto the lake. He wanted to demonstrate His divine nature by walking to them on the water.

Many Christians and churches have been put in the same situation today. They row hard, but they cannot seem to make headway. God is giving them a thirst for His glory by contrasting it with the drudgery of church without His glory. He wants them to put their faith in Him—not in their own efforts.

If that's where you are—facing stiff opposition, rowing hard, straining every muscle in your body but unable to fight your way to the other shore—don't worry. His glory is on the way!

On the other hand, be sure that when His glory appears, you don't mislabel it as the disciples did. He was about to pass by them, but when they saw Him walking on the lake, they thought He was a ghost. They cried out, because they all saw Him and were terrified.

Some churches today misidentify the move of God and cause Him to remove His glory. How many preachers have you heard speak out against revival, calling it "false," "excessive," "Satan-inspired" or "wrong-headed"? When men rebuke God's visitation, they cause Him to remove His glory.

> *Immediately he spoke to them and said,*
> *"Take courage! It is I. Don't be afraid."*
> *Then he climbed into the boat with them,*
> *and the wind died down.*
> —Mark 6:50–51

The disciples thought Jesus was a ghost, and as soon as they misidentified Him, Jesus got into the boat, and the demonstration of His glory ceased. That's the last thing you want to happen!

Do you want more of His glory? Do you want it to permeate your life? Then be careful not to let fear or spiritual blindness cause you to misidentify it. Why didn't the disciples recognize Him? They had followed Him for many months. Couldn't they see His face? Recognize the familiar gait? How could they suddenly be so spiritually blind?

Mark gives us the commentary at the end of this story: The disciples' hearts were hard, and they didn't understand the miracle of the loaves and fishes. Many churches are in the "loaves and fishes" time today, living in the midst of great miracles but having hearts that don't understand the miracles' significance. They are in danger of missing the glory of God if they stay skeptical or fearful. If we miss what God did yesterday, we won't get what He does today. And if we miss today's glory, we'll miss tomorrow's.

This is the day of ever-increasing glory. You and I may see the greatest demonstration of glory since the New Testament. Will we build a temple for Him to dwell in? Will our churches become empty vessels or receptacles of His glory?

For the glory to come in greater measure, we must recognize and welcome it.

EVERYTHING ACCORDING TO PATTERN

To get the glory, you have to get the pattern right. Too many believers think that they can build any kind of church they want to build and still convince God to send His glory. But just as it was with the tabernacle and temples in the Old Testament, there is a pattern that welcomes the glory. Any other pattern drives it away.

The heavenly pattern for a local church is not a denominational pattern, an evangelical pattern, a charismatic pattern or a traditional pattern. It's a pattern of what goes on in heaven! It's not the design of you or me, of this or that local church. It's the design of God, and we find the blueprints for it in the Bible.

What is the point of having a church service? Is it to have

a once-a-week shared experience with other Christians? To sing loudly in order to release some of the tension from the workweek? Is it to show our kids that there is something more to life than school and work?

Perhaps you think the reason we have church services is to have quiet time and refocus on core values. Maybe church for you is about making business contacts. Maybe you even see it as a cheap way to be entertained.

Some people are accustomed to watching other people perform, so they think church is a theater event. They find a comfortable pew, watch the show and put a little money in the plate for a good performance. The only thing missing is the popcorn (and I'm sure some pastor somewhere has added even that).

I believe that a church service is much more than any of these things. It is about making a copy of what is in heaven—a place where God is worshiped and where holiness and love reign. It is about building the right kind of temple for God to dwell in. The goal of every local church should be making a place that is comfortable for Him, not for us.

Of course I am not against padded pews or attractive decorations in the sanctuary. I'm not against carpets or nice restroom facilities. But I am vastly more concerned with the divine comforts that invite the Lord. Our job as a church is not to make visitors or members comfortable. Our first goal must be to have a church that God will attend. Our job is to lead people in preparing a place for God to dwell. Visitors are great, and comfort is nice, but nothing can compare to the King!

BASINS, BOWLS AND ALTARS

Of course the heavenly pattern for revival today is nothing like the pattern for the temple in the Old Testament. I'm not recommending we buy oil lamps, basins, bowls and sacrificial altars like those in the Jewish temple. That would be looking back to a temple where God no longer dwells.

The pattern for revival and church life today consists of right attitudes, right motives and a right spirit. The pattern is for hearts that love and are generous to each other. The heavenly pattern is not about building with the proper materials like wood and nails—it's about Christians learning to get along and function as a body.

Most of Paul's letters were written so he could point the early church to the heavenly pattern:

> *If you have any encouragement from being united with Christ, if any comfort from his love, if any fellowship with the Spirit, if any tenderness and compassion, then make my joy complete by being like-minded, having the same love, being one in spirit and purpose. Do nothing out of selfish ambition or vain conceit, but in humility consider others better than yourselves. Each of you should look not only to your own interests, but also to the interests of others.*
> —PHILIPPIANS 2:1–4

Jesus' entire ministry was about teaching people to live as the family of God in the kingdom of God.

> *My command is this: Love each other as I have loved you. Greater love has no one than this, that he lay down his life for his friends.*
> —JOHN 15:12–13

We each must ask ourselves these questions: Do I fit the description they give? Do I have tenderness and compassion toward everyone else? Do I consider others better than myself? Do I actually love others enough to give my life for someone else?

For many people, and many churches, the answers would be no. What some churches call *unity* is really only a shared list of beliefs—not real love for one another. People stand next to each other and relate upward to God, but they never bother to relate to one another in a way that would bring true friendship, unity and love. We break God's pattern for revival when we walk into the sanctuary trying to guard ourselves from being known by other Christians and avoiding commitments and relationships.

One of the wonderful things about heaven is what *isn't* there. There is no lack of commitment. There is no competition. No music minister tries to impress you with his voice or his interpretation of a song. No usher puts on a spiritual face to hide the pride in his heart. No nursery worker lays a guilt trip on you for not volunteering. Nobody looks at his watch and wonders when the pastor will stop preaching. No one withholds his tithe or speaks badly of the pastor on the ride home.

These things break the pattern of heaven. Heaven's pattern is overflowing joy, peace, goodness and love. It is obedience and trusting God. It is the wind of the Holy Spirit filling you with life.

Heaven's pattern is utter reverence for God. There is a pile of crowns at the feet of Jesus that have been placed there by saints who want only His glory. Tossing aside their own crowns, they sing, "Holy, holy, holy, Lord God Almighty." With each movement of His holy presence, revitalizing life flows from Him and envelops His people with His glory!

Heaven's pattern is honor for the King. For that reason, sometimes at our services I bump the salvation prayer to within the first hour. If there are people who don't fit the pattern, I want them to make up their minds for Jesus right up front. That way we don't have to wait—and Jesus doesn't have to wait—until the end of service to get closer to the heavenly pattern.

I see church as a time to honor the most honorable Guest in the universe. Before a president or king arrives in a city, people go to a lot of effort to prepare the right atmosphere. That's what I try to do. I want everything to be suitable for Him. I want the right kind of heart, right kind of attitude, the right kind of music.

It feels so wonderful to focus on Jesus rather than upon other people during a church service! It eliminates the need to concentrate on trying to fix things so the visitors will come, so young people will come, and so the neighborhood will come. I want all those people to come, but most of all I want Jesus to come.

THE FİRST TABERNACLE

Imagine that you went to a builder and asked him to construct a house for you. You already had the plans ready, down to how many bedrooms you wanted, what you wanted the kitchen cabinets to look like and what kind of glass to use in the windows. The builder took the blueprints and said, "Don't worry; leave it to me. I'll call you when it's done."

Several months later the magic day arrived. The builder insisted on driving you blindfolded to the new house so he could get your first reaction. He led you into the foyer, removed the blindfold... and the house was nothing like what you had planned.

Instead of two stories he gave you one story plus a basement. When you ask why, he says, "I figured you needed some storage room instead of an upstairs bedroom."

Instead of granite counter tops he used stainless steel because he thought it matched the tile, which he also changed from a wooden floor. The bedrooms were in totally different places, the bathrooms had the wrong fixtures, and there wasn't even a fireplace. The builder kept some of the original ideas, but he freely substituted his own ideas whenever he felt like it.

You wouldn't want to live in the house. You would demand that he rebuild your house—this time according to your specifications! In the same way, God has a pattern of revival in heaven. It does not include what we like or dislike. It is not negotiable. It is God's pattern, and we must stay true to it.

Hebrews 8:5 says:

> *They [the priests of the Old Testament]*
> *serve at a sanctuary that is a copy and shadow*
> *of what is in heaven. This is why Moses was*
> *warned when he was about to build the*
> *tabernacle: "See to it that you make*
> *everything according to the pattern*
> *shown you on the mountain."*

Moses wrote down all the details that would make the earthly tabernacle like the heavenly one—the basin, the utensils, the altar, the curtains and every last part. Everything had to be just right. Then Moses finished his work, and the glory of God came down and filled the tent.

Moses' work was not to build what he liked or what the craftsmen thought was pretty. His instructions were to build what God told him to build. Anything else would not have led to the end result. God was not going to dwell in something that deviated from the original temple in heaven.

As the high priests of our day, it is our job to keep the heavenly pattern. Rather than using our own pattern that we believe will draw lots of people on Sunday morning because it includes everyone's favorite style of music, doesn't require too much extra time and doesn't ask people to respond to altar calls, we must adhere to the heavenly blueprints.

If we use our own patterns for revival, refusing to recognize the plan of God, our "copies" will eventually become distorted and irrelevant. No ministry or revival has relevance if it doesn't match the shadow. Over the centuries many denominations began pursuing the heavenly pattern only to fall into some other pattern and lose the glory.

The most important thing we can do when we feel the winds of God's Spirit blowing revival in our direction is to be sure we recognize the pattern of revival that He is using.

When God wants us to move in the direction of becoming "one is spirit and purpose," but we want to stay in the early stage of receiving blessings, personal prophecies and basking in the presence of God, we miss the pattern He has chosen. When we think God *owes* us a revival party after years of spiritual dryness, and think a loving God would never put demands on people to forsake their lives to follow His plan, we have moved out of the pattern of heavenly revival.

God's pattern is changing. Any church could fall behind if we insist on sticking with what feels comfortable rather than what God is revealing about the direction of the church.

REAL SPIRITUAL WARFARE

Most churches and pastors today understand that spiritual warfare is an essential part of the ministry of the local church. But I believe that spiritual warfare—like other functions of church life today—must match the pattern of heaven.

The desire to go to war with the devil can become an area where a fleshly spirit of power and control are exhibited—exactly the same spirit Satan had when he was booted out of heaven. In a desire to name and tear down demonic principalities, it is possible to act out of carnal desire for power and independence to the point of feeling we are in charge—and failing to follow the instructions of our Mighty Warrior Commander, Christ Jesus. If we exhibit the same spirit as Satan, we can never cast him out of a person or situation. If we are into spiritual warfare because we don't like to be told what to do, or because we want power, then our motivation is wrong.

It is vitally important to understand what spiritual warfare really is. In 2 Corinthians 10, Paul describes for us the kind of warfare that needs to be waged. This is what he says:

> *I beg you that when I come I may not have to be as bold as I expect to be toward some people who think that we live by the standards of this world. For though we live in the world, we do not wage war as the world does. The weapons we fight with are not the weapons of the world. On the contrary, they have divine power to demolish strongholds. We demolish arguments and every pretension that sets itself up against the knowledge of God, and we take captive every thought to make it obedient to Christ. And we will be ready to punish every act of disobedience, once your obedience is complete.*
> —2 CORINTHIANS 10:2–6

Was Paul talking about the devil? No, he was talking about people in the Corinthian church who thought it was OK to live by the standards of the world. What was the stronghold facing the Corinthian church? It was people who said we can live by the standards of this world. That's what motivated Paul to tell the Corinthians that he had weapons to deal with just that sort of problem.

Some churches love pretending to pull down spiritual strongholds because it takes the focus off the lifestyles of the people and the fact that they are not following the pattern of heaven. People mistakenly believe that they can still live by the standards of this world—and get their spiritual power fix at the weekly spiritual warfare meeting.

If we target the real strongholds, we will need weapons that are not of this world. These weapons will be successful against the real spiritual stronghold gripping people today—which are arguments and every pretension or pattern that sets itself up against the knowledge of God and breaks the pattern of heaven. Paul advised the Corinthians to "take captive every errant thought." He wasn't talking about the devil's thoughts. He was referring to the worldly thoughts within the church that are leading people astray.

The thoughts we are to capture are the arguments that say we should live by the standards of this world. Imagine the power and influence of the godly church that recognizes strongholds that exist inside the building—not the demonic principalities floating invisibly above the city.

OUT OF ORDER

It is also possible to miss the heavenly pattern for revival by misinterpreting what constitutes "decently and in order." Paul wrote, "Everything should be done in a fitting and orderly way" (1 Cor. 14:40).

Through the centuries that passage has been used to stop revival—not to help revival. Many times when God begins to move in power, someone throws out this scripture, saying, "This feels disorderly." Religion traditionally solves problems by removal. If something can't be strictly controlled, religious people attempt to stop it.

Over the years the church has thrown out all sorts of gifts

because they cause problems—healing, prophecy and tongues to name three. It often seems easier to follow our own pattern—just show up, sing a few hymns, get the offering, preach a sermon and send people on their way with no controversy, no clash, no problems—and no growth.

But the point of having the heavenly pattern, which includes the gifts of the Spirit, is to let them be done in order. Paul said to let everything be done, but just make sure it's done in the right way. To do that we have to learn God's order. We need to restore that order to have a church that can receive His glory for years on end, not just days.

Have you ever attended a church that was very different from the type of service with which you were familiar? It was probably very strange to you. Maybe it seemed out of order. But unfamiliarity doesn't always mean disorder.

I remember when our little town of Smithton installed its first soda machine. One night as I drove through town after everything was closed up and dark, I turned a corner and saw a white light shining down the street. It was a soda machine. I was excited. Apparently the onslaught of people attending our revival services had convinced the town to add the machine for the convenience of the visitors.

However, I soon discovered that although the soda machine had a bright light that could be seen at night, there were no soda cans in the machine. It was empty! The Holy Spirit spoke to me about that machine and said, "Some churches are like that. They are all lit up, but they are empty inside. The people come, put in their money, but go away thirsty."

When a soda machine is empty, someone puts up a sign up that says, "Out of order." I began to realize that the church today can be out of order. Without following God's pattern for revival, our own foolish patterns are empty and leave people thirsty for more.

HEİGHT + DEPTH = LENGTH

Some churches err by throwing out all workings of the Holy Spirit. Other churches err by opening their doors to everything because they don't want to miss whatever the Holy Spirit is doing. Either approach leads to an imbalance that shortens revival.

Church is not supposed to be a free-for-all. If a church believes that attempting any kind of order in a service means the Holy Spirit is being restricted, the result is chaos. That is disorder. In the Book of Judges, the Word says, "Every man did that which was right in his own eyes" (Judg. 21:25, KJV). We cannot allow that to happen in our churches today. A God-sent revival doesn't happen just so people can express themselves and exercise their spiritual gifts. Revival is a place where God's glory comes down.

We strive for orderly freedom in our church. For example, we don't let people prophesy spontaneously because we have so many people coming through whom we don't know. We ask people to write down their prophecies and give them to us. (After all, in the Book of Revelation, John was told to write down what he saw. Each of the Old Testament prophets had to do the same.) Through the years people sometimes want to stand up and say what they feel the Lord would have them say, but we consider that out of order because we don't know the people. It may be a sincere person with a great ministry, but there is no way to check that on the fly. If that person should be a witch or someone with a strange spirit, that word would work against the heavenly pattern and our efforts to make a place for His glory. Visitors sometimes forget that we don't know them and that those preaching witchcraft do attend our services, happy to get a chance to express themselves.

I admit that we might miss legitimate words from God sometimes because of our policy, and we are trying to find a better way to filter the sincere people from the insincere. But the point is this: Church is about God's expressing Himself, not us expressing ourselves to each other. His glory is worth the caution.

Order produces freedom and brings the glory of God. Freedom is not the absence of boundaries. When boundaries are removed, no one knows where the line of demarcation is. Rather than advancing in the things of God, everyone spins their wheels trying to figure out where the lines are located. Boundaries are important, and the Bible gives us a head start on knowing how things work. God's Word gives us safety within parameters.

Church services should be the same way. Only with boundaries can we really enjoy the presence of God. When the power of God first hit our church, we didn't know what to do with it, so we decided to set up boundaries. When it's time to shout, jump or dance, you can do that in any way you want, but when God is moving in conviction, we do that together. Whatever God is doing, we do it together. I have found that He almost always does the same kind of work in everyone at the same time. A wave of conviction will blow over the entire congregation, or a fresh breeze of joy will be felt. I've attended meetings where the preaching of the Word could not be heard because so many people were dancing, yelling or laughing. Some call that freedom; I call it *disorder.* It has been a rare moment when I've been in a service that was working effectively while people in one part of the room were dancing and laughing while those in the other part were on their faces weeping.

When we put order into our revival services, the power of God didn't let up one bit. The Holy Spirit was not offended during the preaching when I felt it was necessary to tell everyone to sit down and listen. If some person decides to grab the spotlight instead of going along with what God is doing, we escort that person to another room to continue what he or she was doing. That way the rest of the congregation is not distracted from what God is doing in the service.

Keeping the right balance often results in lengthening revival—allowing an atmosphere where God can continue to move and change lives. Often pastors call me to say, "We had a wonderful move of God for five or six weeks, and then it shut down."

My response is to ask, "Did God decide it was time to leave?"

As they begin to explain what happened, it usually comes out that every night their services were a sort of "freedom fest," with people being allowed to do whatever they felt like doing. Revival is not an opportunity for mass self-expression—it is an opportunity for God to express Himself through people who live within the boundaries of His will. If God is not allowed to express Himself, after a while people will actually be driven away by the chaos and man-centeredness of the services.

When God is allowed to express Himself, He not only reveals His glory, but He begins to deal with the deepest root of who we are. Then revival becomes well rounded, touching every aspect of who we are and what we need to become. I like to put it in an equation:

$$Height + Depth = Length$$

Height represents God revealing Himself to us in power and glory. Those are wonderful moments of elation and epiphany when heaven seems so close. Depth represents God revealing us to us. These are moments when we grieve over our sin and acknowledge how far from Him we are. Length represents when both of those things are happening in the right balance. The result is that we sustain a long move of God, and the pattern becomes more like heaven.

SENDİNG İT UP

There is a trend in many churches today to cut back on the length of services to fit busy lifestyles. That always means cutting back on the time spent sending praises up to God. It is important for us to understand that cutting back on our "sending up" time means cheating ourselves of God's "coming down" time.

At our church we spend a lot of time preparing, preaching and training ourselves how to send up praises to God. We know the biblical pattern for revival teaches that there is a direct correlation between the amount of glory coming down and the amount of praise going up. If you'll increase what goes up, you'll increase what comes down.

What do we send up? We offer up praise, thanksgiving, honor, worship. We ascribe to God what is due Him, and He responds by lovingly coming down and filling our presence with glory. But it doesn't happen if we walk into church and stand quietly waiting for it. It's interactive. We have to take steps toward Him, as the Bible says:

Come near to God and he will come near to you.
—JAMES 4:8

We want God to know He is welcome, so we do our best to tell Him with our mouths, our bodies and our hearts. I believe God looks at all three expressions to see if we fit the pattern.

Some people want to have the glory without changing their heart or praise habits to fit the pattern. They want to sit in on a good service, sing a few good songs, hear a good sermon and then watch heaven come down. The problem is, they haven't really sent anything up. If you want to experience more of God's glory, increase the amount of praise you send up to Him.

A PLACE FOR HIS FEET

My goal is to change patterns immediately when I discover something in our church that doesn't yet conform to heaven's pattern. I want everything we do to follow God's pattern implicitly—100 percent of the time. If God reveals more of His heavenly pattern to me at midnight on a Saturday night, I guarantee it will be in place Sunday morning—not a week later after I've had time to think about it. I won't wait to think up an explanation or theory as to why the pattern is the way it is. It will be in place the following Sunday morning without warning. No one gets a warning when God makes demands. A warning is a luxury.

One of the pressures of revival can be the need to perform, to make things happen again—in essence, to follow the pattern of people's expectations. As a pastor I have to be very careful not to try and make something happen for the sake of people. I have had people come to a service and tell me, "So-and-so brought his cousin from out of state, and she's really hoping to get healed." I may want her to get healed, too, but I would never falsely say something like, "God is sending a wave of healing," unless it was true. I must do only what pleases the Lord—even if that person leaves the meeting disappointed.

We should all have that attitude. We should not praise or lift our hands to impress or please somebody. And we should not refuse to praise or lift our hands so as not to embarrass somebody. Let's learn to focus completely on God as we enter His sanctuary. The point of all our corporate times together should be to make the Lord comfortable. In Isaiah 66:1 we read:

Heaven is my throne, and the earth is my footstool.

I have taken that passage to heart. God wants a place to put up His feet, and earth is that place. My job is to make a comfortable footstool for Him. I want my church to be a place of rest, where He doesn't have to fight bad attitudes or prejudices or tummy clocks. In our services, I want Him to feel the same as He feels in heaven.

Other churches feel the same way and are trying to copy the heavenly pattern as it is revealed to them. Pretty soon the face of the earth will be covered with thousands of footstools for God, places where His glory can reside.

Your life can be a footstool for God. Your home, church and neighborhood can, too. As you practice the heavenly pattern correctly, the glory you experience in church and individually will grow more brilliant.

FOURTEEN

JESUS SAW YOU FIRST

When we moved the church to Kansas City we didn't follow the pattern perfectly, and we paid a price for that. I sincerely wanted to do everything right, but at key points I chose a pattern tailored to men's expectations and logic, not the plan God had for us.

But once we returned to the original plan to buy property and build on our own piece of land, there was an immediate increase in the fruit of our ministry. I was amazed by the dramatic upturn in people being saved and healed. Obedience had its rewards.

It began after the K-Mart debacle, when I finally reconsidered the idea of buying property. In a way God forced my hand—there were no more buildings available to lease! During that time I was so thankful for people who wrote from all over the country to say, "Don't quit. We need this revival." Finally, I felt that we were on the right track again.

When we first looked for property to buy, I inquired about a five-acre piece of property that was ideal for us, but which cost ten million dollars. When we started looking again a year later, I noticed that across the highway from the five-acre parcel was a sixty-two-acre parcel. Simple math told me that it would probably cost twelve times what the five-acre parcel cost—definitely out of our budget! But the more times I drove by, the more endeared I became to it. After a while, even though we didn't really mean to, Kathy and I started to call it "our land."

Out of curiosity I sent one of our staff members to look around the property. He walked all over it and called me from his cell phone with a report. He said it was good land that would easily accommodate a sanctuary, office building and parking lot. Everything we ever needed and hoped for could be done on the land, he said, and there would be plenty of wooded space to spare.

But there was one problem: Someone already had a contract on it, and by all appearances it was sold. Again I felt deflated. We began to scope out other possibilities, but nothing stuck in my heart like those sixty-two acres.

One day, the staff member who had been spying out the land for me called with a surprise. The contract on the land had fallen through, and it was for sale again. I started to rejoice like a man who had won the lottery. Not only was "our land" up for sale again, it was still zoned for agriculture rather than commercial use, meaning it would cost much less than the properties around it. If we could buy it before it was rezoned, we could get it for the same amount of money that land sold for back in the cornfields of Smithton. Could this really be the time things would go right?

Even with the lower price, the land was still more than we could afford, but we decided to take a leap of faith. A series of miracles of generosity made it possible. Not long after that, I got a call from Pat Robertson, whom Kathy and I had known for several years.

"Steve, I've been in three days of prayer and fasting, and you came to my mind," he said. We talked about what was happening with the property, and he said, "When you get into that tent, expect miracles to increase." And they did. Pat came to visit several months later. We stood on the concrete slab that had been poured, and together we prayed that God would use the property to spread revival around the world.

But first we enjoyed several months in a revival tent.

TESTING IN THE TENT

One of the most challenging times for us as a church was the six months we spent meeting in a tent on our newly purchased property. If we hadn't felt so blessed at having our own property right on the highway, it might have been a much drearier time. It turned into a time of celebration and bonding as we overcame more unexpected obstacles.

We held our first meeting there in late June with no electricity, no bathrooms and no offices—only a 1,000-seat tent and some folding chairs. Soon we hauled in portable toilets and office trailers and hooked up electricity so we could run a sound system.

Healings increased on that very first night. In fact, they tripled.

We started drawing large crowds from across America, but the weather made things interesting from the start. We had the hottest summer on record in Kansas City, which forced us to buy six ten-ton air conditioners and try our best to seal off the tent so it stayed cool. On Labor Day weekend it was 110 degrees. We tried putting a tarp over the tent and wetting it down, but that only worked a little—and it leaked. So we bought silver tarps and put them over the tent;

they worked much better. The only thing breaking up the monotony of the heat was summer storms, which brought hail and high winds that blew the tent flaps.

By the months of November and December, we were locked into the coldest winter in the history of Kansas City and the Midwest. One night I pulled my car onto the property, and the dashboard temperature gauge read minus five degrees. I sat there thinking, *What are we going to do? Are people going to come?*

They did come, and we turned those air conditioners into heaters. We were tested by the weather, but we didn't cancel any services. People came, and God blessed us.

At the same time we were trying to build a building on the property. With winter bearing down on us, people worked all night long. We had no choice. Finally, after six months in the tent, the foyer was finished so we crammed people in there. A few weeks later we moved into the sanctuary.

Oh, the relief! How wonderful it was to be out of the tent, in our own facility, on the right path once again. But despite the challenges of those months of transition, we learned that following the fire produces wonderful, lasting fruit. By being obedient and sticking to the pattern God gives you for your life, you can reach a place of great fruitfulness.

WHO CHOOSES WHOM?

I don't think we could have stuck it out if we hadn't known that God chose us for this hour in history, just as He has chosen you and your church. There is something powerful about knowing God personally selected you.

All my life I have heard about people "choosing" Christ, "making decisions" for Christ and "giving their lives" to Him as if the entire motive lay with us. When I began reading the Gospels as a young man, I realized that we didn't choose Jesus—He chose us. Salvation is not about discovering God, as if He was sitting there waiting for us to notice Him. It is about giving in to the choice He already made to call us.

Not only did He choose us first, but He has a legitimate claim upon our lives. He owns the first rights. We don't follow Him because it sounds like a good idea. We follow Him because He saw us first. In John's Gospel, we see a beautiful portrait of this truth in the story about Jesus' causing a stir among a certain group of men:

> Philip found Nathanael and told him,
> "We have found the one Moses wrote about in
> the Law, and about whom the prophets also
> wrote—Jesus of Nazareth, the son of Joseph."
>
> "Nazareth! Can anything good come from there?"
> Nathanael asked.
>
> "Come and see," said Philip.
>
> When Jesus saw Nathanael approaching,
> he said of him, "Here is a true Israelite, in whom
> there is nothing false."
>
> "How do you know me?" Nathanael asked.
>
> Jesus answered, "I saw you while you were still
> under the fig tree before Philip called you."
>
> Then Nathanael declared, "Rabbi, you are
> the Son of God; you are the King of Israel."
>
> Jesus said, "You believe because I told you I saw
> you under the fig tree. You shall see greater things
> than that." He then added, "I tell you the truth,
> you shall see heaven open, and the angels of God

ascending and descending on the Son of Man."
—JOHN 1:45–51

This little glimpse into the early days of Jesus' ministry illustrates one of the basic principles of justice. Any little boy or girl can tell you what it is: If you had something first, it belongs to you. That goes for toys, land, automobiles, antiques, girlfriends, boyfriends, seats at the restaurant and anything else that inspires competition between people. If you had it first, nobody else can claim it. End of case.

That is essentially what Jesus told Nathaniel: "I saw you first. You were biding your time under a fig tree, but I had a plan for your life before you even knew who I was."

That can be said of you, too. No matter who has put a claim on your life, what job demands your time or what career goals you consider most important, Jesus saw you first. He saw you while you were biding your time. He saw you before the world began. He is so interested in you that even though the earth had yet to be formed—the oceans and the trees and all the universe and the moon and the stars and the sun—Jesus was looking at you. He chose you, as He told the disciples:

You did not choose me, but I chose you and
appointed you to go and bear fruit—fruit that will last.
—JOHN 15:16

Today we don't catch all the implications of that statement. Back then rabbis did not choose their students, but students chose their teacher. Where did John the Baptist get his disciples? Young men came to him and said, "I want to be your disciple." John didn't recruit them. He couldn't demand that someone follow him.

But when Jesus wanted disciples, He hunted them down and handpicked them.

All your life you have been like John's disciples, choosing

whom and what you wanted to follow. Then along comes Jesus, and instead of waiting for you to choose Him, He points the finger at you and says something amazing: "I chose you already. Follow Me." Whether or not you obey, He still has first rights to your life.

Some people live their whole lives knowing they have been chosen, but never responding. They push it down, cover it up, eat and drink a lot and fill their lives with entertainment so that they almost don't notice the call of God in their heart. Then they get around somebody who is following the call, and it starts eating at them. They dismiss it: "I can't do anything about it now. I have so many obligations, so many people to whom I owe money, so many people to whom I have made promises."

But God says, "Wake up! I saw you first. Leave that other stuff behind and follow the call."

Don't be like Nathaniel—stuck under a fig tree. Don't settle for the shade and refuse to budge. Don't become accustomed to the ease, the pace, the rest. Don't define your life by filling up on figs and sleeping in the afternoon. Life is so much more than that! Jesus told Nathanael:

> *You believe because I told you I saw you under the fig tree. You shall see greater things than that . . . I tell you the truth, you shall see heaven open, and the angels of God ascending and descending on the Son of Man.*
> —JOHN 1:50–51

There is much more for us than eating figs and resting in the shade. Jesus promises that when we follow Him we will see amazing things that blow our minds. Live your life to see heaven open. Then you will be able to gaze on the Lord in His glory just as Nathanael did when he stood to his feet and left the fig tree life behind.

NEHEMİAH

In Nehemiah we have a portrait of a person who left fig-tree living behind. Nehemiah had been taken captive to Babylon like hundreds of other children of Israel, and he became the cupbearer to the king. He was so well known by the king that one day the king noticed that Nehemiah was not his usual, cheery self.

Stuck in a foreign palace as cupbearer to a foreign king, Nehemiah was living a fig-tree existence. He had a good job in the king's palace. He was close with the king and took part in all the luxuries of royal living. Anyone observing Nehemiah's position would have said, "Nehemiah, stay with it! Keep the job, hold the cup for the king, take little vacations here and there and enjoy yourself." But something in Nehemiah was bigger than that, and it caused him to give up his cozy life. Nehemiah decided to leave the shade tree.

He went to one of his brothers and asked what was happening in Jerusalem. His brother told him that those who survived the overthrow at the hands of the Babylonians were still living there, but they were in great trouble and disgrace. The wall of Jerusalem was broken down, and its gates had been burned with fire.

When Nehemiah heard these things he sat down and wept. Something stirred in his soul. Like fireworks on the Fourth of July, the call of God erupted on the inside, and he didn't even know how to respond. So he did what we all would do—he cried.

Even before Nehemiah recognized the call of God in his life, God saw Nehemiah first. He gave him a purpose before Nehemiah had any inkling of it. But it took leaving the shade of the tree and heading back to Jerusalem.

LET'S REBUİLD THE WALL

This is the day to rebuild God's kingdom. All it takes is

one cupbearer who will make a difference. Someone needs to say, "That's it. I'm not going through my existence taking drinks to the king anymore. I don't care about my retirement plan, my fishing pole or my RV. The stirrings of God are in my soul, and I'm not going to spend the rest of my life under the shade of a fig tree."

Yes, it's wonderful that God saw you under the fig tree. But that's not your destiny. Your destiny is to see heaven open. To live with heaven above your head, not a fig tree above your head. Some Christians today have plenty of figs, but not very much heaven. It's going to take some cupbearers to leave the life of luxury and say, "We're going to rebuild the church the way God intended it to be."

When some people pray, "Lord, give me the double portion," what they are really asking for is a double portion of fig trees!

But the Lord responds by saying, "OK, I want you to rebuild the church to have a massive, world-changing revival." The double portion that is being handed out to people all over the world is the double anointing to rebuild the church and structure it according to the pattern of heaven.

One of the unique things about many revivals today is that nobody came from the outside to make them happen. Nobody strategized or sought out big-name preachers or hired worship leaders. There were no revival committees, no board meetings, no planning sessions. People simply let God come down and work through them. They let the cupbearers arise from within their congregation. They welcomed the Nathanaels who had been sitting under the fig trees but decided they wanted more than that.

Don't miss a move of God because you're waiting for God to send somebody else. God is calling you. Hear Him saying to you, "I saw you first."

WASTE YOUR LİFE

The people of his day probably thought Nehemiah had wasted his life. Some of Nathanael's relatives probably thought that, too.

But *waste* is a relative term. Just as Paul switched the definitions of loss and gain after he met Christ, so Nehemiah and Nathanael realized that what seemed to be a wasted life was actually the only kind of life worth living.

One of Jesus' disciples once accused Jesus of being wasteful. He responded by teaching His disciples a lesson about responding when the right season was upon them.

*While Jesus was in Bethany in the home
of a man known as Simon the Leper, a
woman came to him with an alabaster jar of
very expensive perfume, which she poured on his
head as he was reclining at the table. When the
disciples saw this, they were indignant. "Why
this waste?" they asked. "This perfume could
have been sold at a high price and
the money given to the poor."*

*Aware of this, Jesus said to them,
"Why are you bothering this woman? She has
done a beautiful thing to me. The poor you will
always have with you, but you will not always have
me. When she poured this perfume on my
body, she did it to prepare me for burial.
I tell you the truth, wherever this gospel
is preached throughout the world, what
she has done will also be told, in
memory of her."*

—MATTHEW 26:6–13

Was this gesture extravagant? Yes. Modern scholars figure that the perfume was worth about a year's wages. But this woman recognized that the season they were in, which led up to Jesus' burial, was unique and required a magnanimous response.

The lesson is this: Don't squander the special times God gives to us. Give everything you have to them. "Waste" your life on them.

Our generation is being blessed with revival, and yet it's still easy to get sidetracked and say we should be doing other things or "balancing" our life with the work of God. People on the outside might say, "What a waste! All this time you could have been enjoying your weekends and going to the beach, going to the ballpark or to the mall. But all you did is go to church."

The best response is, "I'll always have time. I had it growing up; I went to the malls, the ballgames, I goofed off, wasted time, indulged. I'll be able to do that again someday if I want to, but not now. Because now is a time of visitation."

There are really just two choices: You can waste your life on Jesus, or you can waste it on yourself. Judas, who made the accusation of wastefulness against Jesus, decided to waste his life on himself. He poured himself out for his own gain.

Paul, on the other hand, spent his life for Jesus.

> *But even if I am being poured out like*
> *a drink offering on the sacrifice and service*
> *coming from your faith, I am glad and rejoice*
> *with all of you.*
> —PHILIPPIANS 2:17

When you pour yourself out you create a memory that will last forever. Mary, who poured the perfume on Jesus, did not know it, but her moment of extravagant generosity would be captured forever in the Gospel accounts.

How many of us are going to be forgotten forever? Every day you see people who pour themselves out for their jobs, their hobbies, their cars, their vacations, their homes and lawns and other things that disappear in the mists of time. Their lives will be forgotten by all but a few.

But if they choose to waste their life on Christ, it will be a memorial—not just on earth, but in heaven, forever.

CALLING ALL JARS

There is another story in the Bible of a woman with jars of oil, and this one shows us that revival is for everyone who is empty enough to receive it.

In 2 Kings 4 we read:

> *The wife of a man from the company of the prophets cried out to Elisha, "Your servant my husband is dead, and you know that he revered the LORD. But now his creditor is coming to take my two boys as his slaves."*
> —2 KINGS 4:1

In those days, if a man died while owing money to another person, that person could require that a family member become his slave in order to pay off the debt of the deceased. This man's creditor was coming to take his two boys away, which would leave his widow destitute.

> *Elisha replied to her, "How can I help you? Tell me, what do you have in your house?"*
> —2 KINGS 4:2

That's our first lesson: God will always use what you have, not what you lack. Instead of looking at the call on your life from the lack side—"I lack anointing, I lack spiritual discernment, I lack the gift of healing"—look from the supply side. Do you need musicians in your church? Ask if there is anyone who can carry a tune. Is there someone who has ever taken guitar lessons? Do you want to start a media ministry? Ask if anybody has ever worked a video camera or taken broadcast lessons in college. That strategy has worked for us, and God has honored it. When we need something, we look within our own congregation.

That's what Elisha did. When the widow said she had nothing except a little oil, Elisha decided to let God work through that oil first.

I see many people pray for great anointing, and that's well and good, but I wish they would pray *and* allow God to work through them by using what they already have. There are thousands who have gone through Bible colleges and Bible studies and been prayed for by the greatest ministers in the world who are sitting around waiting for God to launch their ministries. I know of one particular Bible school whose graduates tend to settle in the same city, as many as four thousand of them; it appears they're all waiting for their worldwide ministries to hit them on the head.

Meekness is expressed by allowing God to bless what you are now. There are people in my church who have been greeters for a long time, and I don't know if they ever get thanked. Not many people pray, "God, anoint me to be a greeter. I've dreamed all my life of greeting people." Yet that's what we needed. Be satisfied with the place God has given you in His body, and let Him promote you at His will.

Only after you use what you have can you start to gather what you don't have. It was after the woman in our story had poured her oil in all the empty jars that she had that she sent her sons out of the house to ask her neighbors for empty jars. This story teaches us to think big. Instead of asking for a few, ask for every empty jar in their house!

Why? Because that kind of faith will be rewarded.

The story ended this way:

> *"Then go inside and shut the door behind
> you and your sons. Pour oil into all the jars, and as
> each is filled, put it to one side." She left him and
> afterwards shut the door behind her and her sons.
> They brought the jars to her and she kept pouring.
> When all the jars were full, she said to her son,
> "Bring me another one." But he replied, "There is
> not a jar left." Then the oil stopped flowing.*
>
> —2 KINGS 4:6

Revival starts with empty jars. That confuses people. They may think, *I have so many things wrong with me, and when I get all that fixed up I'll join revival,* but it's the empty jar that God is looking for.

GET EMPTY BEFORE FİLLİNG UP

You can't fill someone who never became empty. A lot of people are afraid to let their lives run on "E." Sometimes when I'm driving with my family, I let the gas gauge go on "E" just to see if we can make it to the next gas station. Kathy tells me, "Please, I'm not in the mood for another adventure. Let's just go to the gas station up here and buy some gas." It's not a perfect analogy, but as human beings, we have to be willing to trust God enough to let our lives go down to "E" so that we can be filled.

When people receive prayer, one person might get a sudden touch from God while the person next to him gets nothing. What's the difference? One has a full tank, the other an empty tank. Check your gauges. Are you too full of yourself and your world to receive? Jesus spent time with people whose tanks were on "E"—including sinners, prostitutes and tax collectors. Their lives had run down to nothing.

They were running on fumes, and they wanted to be filled.

Spiritually, I still get on "E" sometimes. I preach so much that my gauge drops, and then I have to fill up. It's the most beautiful thing to me to know that although I've been in this move of revival so many years, I still need to be filled again—over and over. Scripture says, "Be ye filled with the Holy Spirit," meaning, "Be continually filled."

Philippians 2:7 says that Jesus made Himself nothing. In other words, He emptied Himself. All the rights that were given to Him as the Son of the living God, He didn't exercise. Have you ever emptied yourself of your rights?

What do you suppose was going on for those three days when God struck Saul blind and he ended up at Ananias' house? Everything—the years of training and study—was draining out. Paul's tank was heading toward "E."

Some people and churches go backward because they start trying to fill up their emptying spiritual tanks by improving self-esteem, practicing self-love and attempting self-improvement. They are fearful of reaching "E." They turn the Bible into a self-improvement book. Jesus wants to change what you are into something else. Instead of trying to fill your own spiritual tank, let it get to "E." Let God fill it up for you.

Do you want to be being filled continually? Stay on empty!

OUR GRATEFUL RESPONSE

God took the initiative in your life. He saw you under the fig tree before you knew Him, before you loved Him. While we were yet sinners Christ died for us. He took the first step. Isn't that amazing?

He saw us first—and He still loved us.

How do we respond? Respond with a grateful heart... with a willingness to work. With the knowledge that He has first rights to our lives. Be a generation of Nathanaels and Nehemiahs. Let's leave the luxuries and fig trees behind for a life of adventure that we can't even comprehend. Let's follow the fire wherever it leads. Let's get the pattern of church right and watch His glory come down.

It's the least we can do for our King. He saw us first— and I am forever grateful.

CONCLUSION

I'm so excited to be alive right now. I'm thankful to be living in this generation, to see the day of His power and to have dreams come true right before my eyes.

But it doesn't come without effort or energy, without prayer or without cost—and it will not come to everyone, because not everyone is willing.

Are you willing? Have you tasted the sweetness of this revival and hungered for more?

This is the day to say yes to God, to take on His identity, to narrow down your options and to leave the shade of the fig tree. It is the day to become a soldier, to use your voice for His glory and to build a church that will be able to receive the glory He wants to send.

Make sure you are part of this move of God, no matter what it takes. Lose as much as you can, empty yourself, strain for the finish line, and you will find a prize worth far more than what you gave up. Revival is now. Will you be part of it?

OTHER REVIVAL RESOURCES
BY PASTOR STEVE GRAY

Book

When the Kingdom Comes by Steve Gray brings part one of the story of a small-town pastor struck by the power of God, igniting a world-renown outpouring of God's presence and power. The exciting lessons learned contain step-by-step biblical principles to obtaining and maintaining a move of God in the local church.

Video

Go Inside the Smithton Outpouring dramatically presents the sights and sounds of a move of God that has affected millions all around the world. Numerous testimonies have been received of how this video has sparked revival in other churches.

Audio and Video Sermon Tape Series

Steve Gray's messages have a prophetic edge that helps to bring the fire of revival and the Word of the kingdom into listeners' hearts.

Music

When Heaven Came Down features original music by Steve Gray. The CD includes "Return to the Lord" and other songs birthed in this revival.

For additional information about the ministry
of Pastors Steve and Kathy Gray, contact:

WORLD REVIVAL CHURCH
9900 View High Drive
Kansas City, MO 64134
Phone (toll free): 1-877-804-LIFE (5433)
E-mail: wrc@wrckc.com
Website: www.worldrevivalchurch.org

IF YOU ENJOYED
FOLLOW THE FIRE,
here are some other titles from
Charisma House that we think will minister to you…

THE BLOOD *and* THE BLOOD STUDY GUIDE
Benny Hinn

ISBN: 0-88419-783-8 (book)   *Retail Price: $13.99 (book)*
ISBN: 0-88419-428-0 (study guide)   *Retail Price: $13.99 (study guide)*

This revised edition of THE BLOOD *offers an opportunity to find the kind of freedom for which every heart longs. The companion interactive workbook provides lessons inviting readers to incorporate what they've learned into their faith walk. These tools are perfect for individual spiritual growth, Bible study, small group or Sunday school.*

THE NATURE OF GOD
David Yonggi Cho

ISBN: 0-88419-773-5
Retail Price: $13.99

Pastor of the largest church in the world, David Yonggi Cho has done an excellent job of explaining the three components of God and expressing the concepts of mercy, grace and redemption. THE NATURE OF GOD *is an excellent discipleship tool that can be used with young or mature believers.*

TAKING OUR CITIES FOR GOD
John Dawson

ISBN: 0-88419-764-8
Retail Price: $13.99

This book invites you to take part in a spiritual clean-up program that will change you and your community forever! TAKING OUR CITIES FOR GOD *offers a revised and detailed action plan that will open the heavens and allow God's blessings to flow freely.*

To pick up a copy of these titles, contact your
local Christian bookstore or order online at
www.charismabookwarehouse.com.